English Brickwork

Ronald Brunskill *and*
Alec Clifton-Taylor

English Brickwork

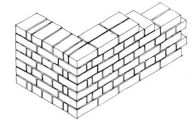

A Hyperion Book
Ward Lock Limited · London

© Ronald Brunskill and Alec Clifton-Taylor 1977

ISBN 0 7063 5087 1

A Hyperion Book
First published in Great Britain in 1977 in association with Peter Crawley
by Ward Lock Limited, 116 Baker Street, London, W1M 2BB,
a member of the Pentos Group.

Designed by Humphrey Stone

Text in Monophoto Plantin

Filmset and printed in England by
Cox & Wyman Ltd, London, Fakenham and Reading

Contents

Acknowledgments

The authors wish to thank the following for kind permission to reproduce photographs of which they hold the copyright: Ronald Adams Associates (*illustration nos*: 30, 31, 33, 151), B. T. Batsford Ltd (2, 5), Mervyn Blatch (7, 12, 23, 25, 36, 122, 133, 140), The Marquess of Cholmondeley (122), Peter Crawley (3, 4, 6, 9, 14, 22, 26, 27, 29, 32, 34, 35, 43, 51, 63, 66, 73, 104, 143, 148), the Gladstone Pottery Museum (144), F. L. Harris (15, 16, 20, 24, 82, 124, 128, 132), Grant Muter (87, 92), Dr J. E. C. Peters (135), Colin Reiners (136), Mrs Edwin Smith (11, 21). The following illustrations are from the National Monuments Record and are Crown Copyright: 1, 8, 10, 13, 17, 28, 55, 67, 68, 80, 89, 90, 95, 99, 100, 101, 102, 103, 105, 106, 107, 108, 110, 111, 112, 113, 117, 118, 119, 120, 123, 125, 126, 127, 129, 130, 131, 134, 138, 139, 146, 149. The remaining illustrations consist of photographs and drawings by R. W. Brunskill.

In assembling the illustrations the authors wish particularly to thank the Curator and staff of the National Monuments Record for help on many occasions, Professor E. S. Benson of the School of Architecture, Manchester University, for permission to reproduce photographs which are part of the School's collections, and Geoffrey Wheeler for his technical skill. Thanks are also due to David Sekers, Curator of the Gladstone Pottery Museum, and to Mervyn Blatch for much help with regard to the illustrations.

For helpful comments on the text the authors are grateful to Professor Jack Simmons and A. S. Ireson.

Warm thanks are also due to Peter Crawley for his enthusiasm and good humour and for his unflagging encouragement.

Introduction

FOR OVER fifty years the indispensable book for every student of our native brickwork has been Nathaniel Lloyd's *History of English Brickwork*, which originally appeared in 1925. But Lloyd included scarcely anything later than 1800, and since 1925 not only have countless millions of bricks been laid: nearly two centuries of brickwork disregarded by him have become worthy of study. More recent books have either dealt with brickwork as one among a number of building materials or have been confined to one period or aspect of the subject, usually with the needs of the prospective architect or apprentice bricklayer as the primary consideration.

Moreover, Lloyd's *History* is a large and expensive book which, even were it still available, could not be conveniently used in the field. It was therefore felt that the time was ripe for a new book which, by word, diagram and illustration, would show how bricks have been used at different periods and in various parts of the country from the earliest times up to the present day. Although it is hoped that this book will be read with enjoyment at home, it is also intended for use on the spot, and in the industrial towns of the North no less than in the cathedral cities of the South. With this aim in mind there is a special appendix describing a simple method of systematic recording, which should enable the user to build up quite quickly a general picture of the brickwork of a particular town or district.

The first part of the book surveys the history of English brickwork throughout the centuries. The various clays and methods of firing, the bonding, the mortar, the virtuosity of the craftsmen of the later seventeenth and early eighteenth centuries and the evolution of substitute materials are all explained and illustrated by reference to examples familiar and unfamiliar: a feature of the book is the number of little-known brick buildings which are referred to and illustrated.

This is followed by a glossary in which illustrations and drawings have been freely introduced to assist in the elucidation of the terms used in brickwork, many but not all of which are still in current use. Terms applicable to building materials in general and not peculiar to brickwork have mostly been excluded. On the other hand bonding, the arrangement of bricks for strength and for ornament, has been treated in some detail.

The third part of the book has photographs arranged in chronological sections, but with special attention to periods and types of building in which brick was particularly popular. As the examples chosen are almost all external views, most of them can be easily seen by the public, but it must be emphasized that a few of the houses illustrated are private property and not accessible without prior permission.

This section includes a few Welsh buildings, for brickwork in Wales, because of its scarcity before the nineteenth century, is apt to be overlooked, but is not without interest. In both England and Wales, here and throughout the book, it has been thought better to maintain the old county names, on which a vast store of architectural and topographical literature is based, rather than to take cognizance of changes introduced in 1974 purely for administrative convenience, without any regard for tradition or for historic loyalties.

In addition to the appendix referred to above, there is another devoted to the growth in popularity and recent decline of the cavity wall, which must unfortunately rank as the most characteristic contribution of the past fifty years to the brick-builder's craft.

Despite the development within the present century of a number of materials new to architecture, brick still continues to play a very important part, particularly for domestic building. It is probable that most people still continue to prefer brick to any other material for their new house. In addition, there is our tremendous heritage of brick architecture from the past. No excuse, therefore, seems necessary for a book which is designed specifically to aid the observation of good brick buildings of every period and to stimulate, it is hoped, an even greater appreciation of them.

One

Brickwork in England

I HAVE often wondered why committing indiscretions should be described as 'dropping bricks'. The choice of bricks seems quite unaccountable, for it is difficult to think of any substance more respectable. Just a lump of clay, kneaded, moulded, given a simple form, rectangular on face, which, after high-temperature baking, could be – and indeed often has been – repeated almost into infinity. Could anything be more innocuous? Boring, even? Then one recalls another common idiomatic use. 'He (or more often she) was a perfect brick.' No hint of indiscretion here: the picture is one of strength, reliability, kindness, warmth. And, if we care for architecture, we may find ourselves asking whether some of our older brick buildings do not embody exactly those qualities.

The word derives almost certainly from the French *brique*. It did not come into general use until the fifteenth century; earlier the current words were *waltyle* (wall-tile) and the Latin *tegula*. Brick can have, as we shall see, other virtues besides those just indicated, yet basically it is a 'utility' material, usually without artistic pretensions, and the large majority of brick buildings, not only in England but in every brick-using country, attract no attention, either in commendation or in condemnation, for their fabric. Only a small proportion is materially of fine quality. But so widespread has been the English preference for brick, which during the last three centuries has been far and away our commonest building material, that even that 'small proportion' embraces countless thousands of structures, mainly houses.

The long and still persisting popularity of brick is not difficult to explain. In the first place, England is very well provided with suitable clays, which occur in almost every geological formation from the alluvial deposits of comparatively recent date as far back as the Carboniferous system, although the shales from the Coal Measures, chiefly associated with Lancashire, Yorkshire, County Durham and Ruabon, just across the Welsh border, could not be used for brickmaking until machines had been invented capable of breaking up these very hard clay rocks and reducing them, after the addition of water, to the required plasticity. More amenable clays have been used by brickmakers in many parts of the country for centuries. Compared with the cost of quarrying and shaping heavy blocks of stone, brick manufacture was cheap, and brickmakers' wages were lower than those of the stonemasons. Cartage was far easier and less expensive, and might even be unnecessary, because it was often possible to dig the clay and set up a small kiln on the site. This is what frequently happened in East Anglia, which is one reason why so many old houses in that part of England are wholly or partly moated, or at least have a pond in the garden.

Standardization of sizes also helped to reduce costs; it always does. In stone this can only be achieved at the cost of aesthetic quality. In brick the opposite is the case: any departure from the standard size looks wrong. So the size of bricks has varied comparatively little through the centuries; the determining factor has always been the size of a man's hand. Because brick is a manufactured article, there has never been any problem about making convenience of handling a prime consideration.

The non-combustibility of brick was another factor which worked strongly in its favour. History abounds in records of timber-built towns being devastated by fire, the most famous instance of all being, of course, the Great Fire of London in 1666. In the seventeenth and eighteenth centuries the rebuilding was always done largely if not wholly in brick, even when there were stone quarries not far away, as at Northampton, Warwick, Blandford, Tiverton and Wareham, to name only a few.

Brick, of course, was ideal for chimney-flues and stacks, and not only timber-framed but even stone houses often resorted to brick for this purpose, as can be well seen at Knole, and all over the town at Malmesbury in Wiltshire, where nearly all the houses are of stone but almost every chimney-stack is of brick.

Comfort was yet another consideration. Being porous, brick is a poor conductor; so a well-built brick house tends to be cooler in summer and warmer in winter than one built in most other materials, including many kinds of stone. In this respect brick is at the opposite pole from glass. This has also operated in its favour except in *avant-garde* circles, where comfort is seldom the first consideration.

Finally there is the question of durability. Provided the right clays have been used and the methods of manufacture have been correct, bricks may endure for centuries, and even outlast many kinds of stone. In particular, brickwork, although it may become grimy and look very unattractive, is impervious to soot and smoke in the atmosphere, which is by no means true of most varieties of limestone. This operated very much in favour of brick in the polluted air of the usual nineteenth-century industrial town.

It will, however, be observed that none of these brick properties has anything much to do with art. Yet England has produced buildings, especially in the southern and eastern parts of the country, which are perhaps the most beautiful ever made in this material. Clearly, therefore, these practical attributes, important though they be, leave out of account all that elevates the craft of the brickmaker, in its finest manifestations, to the status of an art.

The oldest bricks in England date from Roman times, and bear little resemblance to those of later centuries. Roman bricks are broad and thin and usually, because of their thinness, very well burnt, which is the main reason why, generally reused, so many have survived. Dimensions vary, but most of them are no more than $1\frac{1}{2}$ in thick and some as little as 1 in. In length and breadth, on the other hand, they might be twice the size of the modern brick, so are more comparable with tiles. This shape suited the principal purpose for which the Romans employed their bricks, which was as bonding courses introduced at intervals into walls of rubblestone or flint. Although technically good, the Roman product has played no significant part in the story of English brickwork.

Probably because the country was so thickly wooded that there was plenty of timber for everybody, brickmaking ceased with the departure of the Romans, and did not really begin again until the latter part of the thirteenth century. At Little Wenham Hall near Ipswich in Suffolk (*1*), a fortified house of about 1275, flint was used for some of the

1. *Little Wenham Hall, Suffolk:*
   east side

walling and limestone for the dressings, but this is the earliest of our
mediaeval buildings also to incorporate a significant quantity of bricks –
incidentally, of several sizes and colours: cream and greenish-yellow in
greater quantities than the warmer shades. These bricks were almost
certainly baked on the site, but their makers may well have been
Flemings.

From that time onwards, through seven centuries the story of brickwork in England has been one of ever-increasing demand, although for
four hundred years – from the end of the thirteenth century to the last
quarter of the seventeenth century – progress was by no means spectacular. During this long period brick was hardly ever used for cottages
and seldom even for the smaller town houses. Nor was it at all equally
distributed across the country. A map showing the location of brick
buildings of earlier date than 1550 reveals that over half of them are in
Norfolk, Suffolk or Essex, and that nearly all are to the east of a line
drawn from the Humber to the Solent.[1] The reasons were the relative

[1] For this map and much other valuable information about early brickwork, see *Brick Building
in England from the Middle Ages to 1550* by Jane A. Wight (1972).

shortage of building stone, apart from flint, in this part of England and probably also that this was the part of the country most familiar with continental practices; by 1550 there was already a long tradition of brick building in the Netherlands and in the Hanseatic towns.

Early bricks were burnt in 'clamps'. These were just big stacks of dried bricks, daubed outside with clay. Within were layers of fuel, which was usually composed of faggots: bundles of brushwood, tree toppings, hedge splashings and undergrowth generally. Fires were lit from a number of points outside, according to the direction of the wind. In such primitive conditions it was impossible accurately to estimate the right heat needed for firing, so a great many of the bricks produced were imperfect in one way or another. Often, for instance, the surface of mediaeval bricks will be found to show creases: these were produced by sand on the surface of clay being insufficiently puddled. (The puddling process involved squeezing and blending, to produce a smooth 'dough' from which impurities, especially pebbles, had all been removed.) Or, again, in the process of firing one end of a brick might shrink more than the other; this was an irregularity which could be remedied in building by varying the thickness of the mortar. Such technical imperfections do not destroy one's pleasure; although early brickwork will often have a homespun look, these variations may serve to add interest to a wall surface.

So also with colour. Bricks depend for their colour on the chemical nature of the clay itself. Most clays contain a certain amount of iron in their composition, which in the process of firing has the effect of staining the clay red: that is why so many bricks – before the eighteenth century nearly all – are some shade of red. White bricks, so called (for in practice they are always pale yellow, buff or brown), can only be produced naturally when, in addition to iron, the clay contains a relatively high content of lime. (Today lime is sometimes added deliberately.) Other minerals occurring in clays and acting as colouring agents in the furnace include manganese and cobalt, and sand itself is frequently a colouring agent.

Variations of colour in bricks are also produced by the process of firing; even the character of the fuel, in the early days, could make a difference. But the chief factor was the degree of heat. Those bricks exposed to the greatest heat would bake to a darker hue, and perhaps change colour by becoming wholly or partly vitrified. The bricks were always stacked so that the ends and not the sides were burnt the most, and the grey-blue diamond-shaped diapers specially characteristic of the early Tudor period depended on the bricklayers having a sufficient number of burnt ends. It is evident that the supply often ran out, which explains, partly at least, why Tudor diapering is usually so irregular.[1]

In the Middle Ages bonding (which means the way in which the bricks are laid) was usually also somewhat haphazard. In the Tudor period, however, a consistent practice was generally adopted which was to lay the bricks in alternating courses of all stretchers (that is, with only the long sides visible on the wall-face) and all headers (that is, with only the ends exposed). This is the arrangement known as English bond, which in the course of the seventeenth century was gradually to give way to Flemish bond, the method of laying bricks with every course consisting of alternating headers and stretchers.[2] The vital consideration was always the avoidance of straight joints, the term used to describe what happens when there is a vertical joint exactly over another such in the course below. But in addition to this practical reason for bonding, there can be no doubt that bricks laid in a regular fashion give greater aesthetic pleasure.

It was in the secular and especially the domestic sphere that brick first came into its own as a major material of building. There is only a handful of pre-Reformation brick churches; the best are Shelton in Norfolk, a small but choice example of c. 1485–90, Lutton in Lincolnshire and East Horndon, Layer Marney and Chignal Smealy (2), all in Essex. This county also has some Tudor porches, of which the one at Sandon (3) is among the finest, and more than twenty brick towers, Sandon again being a handsome example, although Ingate-

[1] Dr Norman Davey, a distinguished scientist, in *A History of Building Materials* (1961), p. 65, supplies the technical details: 'The majority of clays for brickmaking', he says, 'burn to a red colour when fired at between 900 and 1000 °C, in an *oxidizing* atmosphere. Above this temperature the colour often changes to darker red or purple, then to brown or grey at about 1200 °C. Some clays cannot be heated to such a high temperature as they may melt. . . . In a *reducing* atmosphere in which the supply of oxygen is restricted or cut off, for example by reducing the draught through the kilns, purple-brown or bluish bricks, often with black cores, are produced. The effect of a high iron content in the clay is to produce ferric oxide in an oxidizing atmosphere, making the brick salmon pink at 900 °C and darker red or reddish brown at 1100 °C.'

[2] A recent discovery of considerable interest, not previously recorded, is the employment of Flemish stretcher bond (one course of stretchers alternating with one of headers and stretchers) in England as early as 1563–5. This is at Woodham Walter church in Essex (*104*), where the Elizabethan brickwork was long concealed under rendering (see also p. 27). We are indebted to Mrs Patricia Herrmann for bringing this to our attention.

16

2. *St Nicholas, Chignal Smealy, Essex : window*

3. *St Andrew, Sandon, Essex : south porch and tower*

stone (*4*) is still more imposing. Brick was in fact employed at several much grander churches than these: for the vault-webs of the nave of Beverley Minster as early as the second quarter of the fourteenth century; for the spire of Norwich Cathedral in the 1480s; and for Bell Harry, the central tower of Canterbury Cathedral, a decade or so later. But although the bricks are still there, nearly half a million of them at Canterbury, few people are aware of it, for at Beverley they were plastered over and at both the cathedrals they were faced with lime-stone. The one big church at which, despite renewals, plenty of mediae-val brickwork is still in evidence is Holy Trinity, Hull. The chancel and transepts, built between 1315 and 1345, are the earliest example in the country of brick architecture on anything like a lavish scale.

Nearly all the best examples of secular and domestic architecture of pre-Reformation date in brick are in the East and South-East. To the

17

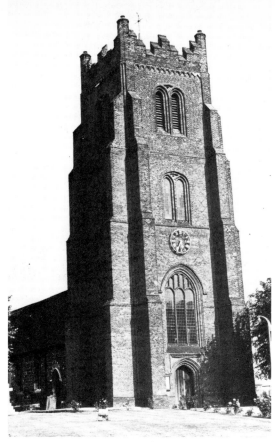

reign of Henry VI belong Herstmonceux Castle (now the Royal Observatory), a grand house, and Tattershall Castle in Lincolnshire, notable for the high quality of its craftsmanship; but unfortunately all that survives there are the tremendous tower (5) and the attractive little gatehouse. The bricks vary in size, but the average is small: about 8 in × 4 in × 2 in. Not long after, another enormous brick tower, more French in aspect, arose at Faulkbourne in Essex. The spiral stair here has a moulded handrail of circular section continued up to the very top, and an excellent tunnel vault. Although the chapel walls were of stone, brick was the principal material employed for Eton College, founded by King Henry in 1440, and at Cambridge several colleges, of which Queens' was the first, were being built in brick before the end of the fifteenth century. So the stage was set for the erection in brick, under Henry VIII, of the largest house in England at that time: Hampton Court Palace. At Tattershall Ralph Cromwell's master-brickmaker had

been a German brought over specially for this job, but before the end of the century English brickmakers were given many opportunities of displaying their skill.

For, although brick might be thought to have imposed various limitations in the direction of plainness, the grander clients were no more willing to eschew 'finish' in brick than they were in stone. A gentleman's house, whether in stone or, now, in brick, was expected to have properly moulded window mullions and transoms, labels or dripstones above the windows (which would not only be moulded but, in the best examples, dropped down a few inches at either side of each window and neatly returned), moulded frames to the doorway arches (and often more: ornamental spandrels, for example), nicely rounded copings to the battlements and gables, and even sunk panels in the walls, crowned by triplets of cusped arches. Sometimes, as at Leez Priory in Essex, erected in 1536–7 on a monastic site by a lawyer appropriately surnamed Rich, these dressings were all of stone. (The splendid inner gatehouse (6) exhibits, according to Miss Jane Wight, 'uniquely complex diapering in blue brick . . . Different sizes of diamonds are supplemented by zigzags, hearts, crosses, chequers, and shades like candelabra and Chinese lanterns.') But elsewhere the brickmakers had to learn how to supply all these requirements, and they would appear to have done so with surprising speed. The gatehouse of Esher Place, now known as Wayneflete Tower, which is all that survives of a house built by Bishop Waynflete of Winchester about 1475–80, has a spiral staircase walled with slightly brownish-red headers, with another finely moulded handrail carried out entirely in brick (7). So has the wonderful gate-tower of Oxburgh Hall in Norfolk, dating from 1482, which is, again, all that remains of the original house. Both of these staircase vaults, in ploughshare forms achieved mainly with stretchers, are extremely accomplished for so early a date.

Some of these ornamental details were so elaborate that they had to be specially prepared, with the aid first of a brick-axe, to reach an approximation of the required shape, and then by laborious rubbing. But wherever possible wooden moulds were employed; if the need was for a quantity of bricks of identical section, this was much the easiest and least expensive method of making them. No more beautiful example of this ornamental brickwork can be seen than on the outer face of the little gatehouse of Giffords Hall, at Stoke-by-Nayland in Suffolk.

6. *Leez Priory, Essex : inner gatehouse*

The most spectacular achievements in brick under Henry VIII were the chimney-stacks. These are of course particularly vulnerable to the weather, and a good many, including all those at Hampton Court, have had to be rebuilt, but a certain number of fine originals still survive. There are many different shapes: octagons, hexagons, squares, circles, or even spirals (*63*), and that is not all, for their surfaces are often adorned with designs in relief. These are also very varied: among them are zigzags, lozenges, diamonds, quatrefoils, honeycombs, Tudor roses and *fleurs de lis* (*8*). Here again, wherever possible, they made

moulds, but it was obviously uneconomic to make a mould for so elaborate and special a detail as the 'Stafford Knot' at Thornbury Castle in Gloucestershire, so this was carved. Usually, however, the various moulded pieces were carefully fitted together as the chimney-stack went up, as can be clearly seen in the close view of the Inner Gatehouse chimneys at Leez Priory (9). Every shaft stands upon a moulded base, and has a projecting cap analogous to the capital that crowns a stone column. Specially thin bricks had to be made for the necking, and also for the 'spurs' which can frequently be seen (though not at Leez Priory) projecting from the angles. Some shafts stand in isolation, but often they are grouped in pairs or fours, and occasionally in greater numbers: at East Barsham Manor in Norfolk, where they used terracotta, there is one group of ten. (Terracotta – from the Latin, *terra cocta* meaning cooked earth – is a term employed somewhat loosely to describe clay of fine consistency mixed with sand and fired to a hardness and compactness seldom attained by brick.)

Under Elizabeth I and James I some very large houses, as well as many smaller, were built mainly or solely of brick: Doddington Hall near Lincoln, Burton Constable (106) and Burton Agnes Hall (10) in the East Riding, Bramshill House (107) in Hampshire, Hatfield House (11) in Hertfordshire, Quenby Hall in Leicestershire (108), Aston Hall, Birmingham and Blickling Hall in Norfolk are among the most outstanding. But despite their size there was a reversion to a greater sobriety in the handling of the brickwork. The north front of Hatfield House, for example, is of studied severity, and aesthetically all the more impressive, surely, on that account: we can understand why this elevation appeals greatly to some architects today.

It was not until the reign of Charles I that a new phase of exuberance developed. This is seen in a group of houses (none of them mansions) built in what Sir John Summerson has aptly termed the Artisan Mannerist style. These buildings – among the most important are the Dutch House in Kew Gardens (12), Broome Park in Kent, Cromwell House at Highgate, and (although not built until 1654) Tyttenhanger in Hertfordshire (117) – do certainly display some remarkable feats in the handling of moulded and carved brickwork. The Dutch

10. *Burton Agnes Hall, Yorkshire, E.R.: south front*

OPPOSITE II. *Hatfield House, Hertfordshire: part of north front*

12. *The Dutch House, Kew, Surrey : south front*

House, for example, has elaborately moulded cornices separating every storey, a tall centre-piece formed by pilasters with capitals, curved gables with moulded copings and at the apex of the gables curved or triangular pediments, deeply moulded (*13*). For these 'dressings' specially fine, soft bricks were required which could be rubbed and cut so precisely that some of the joints were scarcely visible. This was known as gauged work, and it was first developed in the Netherlands; the Dutch House, built in 1631, is our earliest example of it. Moulds were used wherever feasible, but special features like the Ionic and Corinthian capitals on this front had all to be carved. Broome Park, which is a good deal larger than the Dutch House and has much more elaborate gables, is in several respects a still more re-

13. *The Dutch House, Kew, Surrey : south front, detail*

markable example of this virtuosity in the handling of brick. Cromwell House has a fantastic central window, set within a lugged architrave with scrolled consoles, all, it would seem, carved on the spot; but in other respects this front has more classical restraint than the others and, some may feel, is all the better for it. At Tyttenhanger (*14*) the frame of the central window has a segmental pediment, but is otherwise closely similar.

It is generally held that it was at the Dutch House that Flemish bond – as it is called, although, like 'Venetian' windows in Venice, it is not at all common in Flanders – was first used in England.[1] During

---

[1] But see the footnote on p. 16 regarding the use of Flemish stretcher bond in England two generations earlier.

the rest of the seventeenth century it gradually superseded English bond all over the country. Flemish bond is not so strong but is more economical, since the proportion of stretchers to headers is greater and fewer facing bricks are therefore required. The introduction of a number of other bonds followed, one or two about the same time but mostly later: these are described in detail in the Glossary (pp. 67–93). In the Georgian period houses were sometimes faced entirely with headers. One would not want to see nothing else but this, but an example now and again, correctly pointed, always gives pleasure, because of its fine close mesh. This was obviously, for structural reasons, the easiest way of building a curving wall. The continuously curving or serpentine garden wall, sometimes known as a crinkle-crankle, was specially popular in Suffolk in the later Georgian period for the cultivation of slightly tender fruits such as peaches and nectarines. Some of these walls are delightful. The best known, several hundred yards long, abuts on to the main road between Wickham Market and Framlingham (66); unfortunately part of it is now in decay.[1]

The century that followed the Restoration, that is to say from 1660 to 1760, is the period when artistically our brick architecture was at its very finest. Nowhere in the world can more beautiful brickwork be seen than in the best English examples of this age. Because of the superior quality of the clays for brickmaking, and perhaps also because this was the better-off part of the country, it is in the South and East that almost all the most remarkable examples are to be found.

What distinguishes the best brick house-fronts of the later Stuart and early Georgian periods (and I say *fronts* advisedly, for all too often it was a case of 'Queen Anne in front and Mary Anne behind') is the very high level of their craftsmanship, which finds expression in all kinds of different ways. Consider, for instance, the problem of constructing a brick arch. In mediaeval and Tudor times, if recourse were not had to stone (which, if the stone were available, was a nice easy way out), bricks with a chamfer, even a hollow chamfer, or a roll at one end (known today as bullnose bricks) might be specially produced; but often they were not. What happened then was that, using a wooden centering, the arch was constructed with ordinary bricks in a decidedly rough and ready fashion, either by thickening the mortar joints towards its extrados (its outer radius) or by introducing here and there little extra pieces of brick or, sometimes, tile. In some cases this improvisation was decently masked by a thin coat of plaster. With the advent of a more classical type of architecture there was a need for something much more precise. And so they turned to purpose-made bricks and to the gauged rubbers which we have already met performing a different function at the Dutch House.

All these bricks are wedge-shaped, and whether the arch was flat-headed, segmental, semi-elliptical or semi-circular, construction still

[1] Mr Norman Scarfe tells me that for Suffolk his score is now 58. In the whole of the rest of England he knows of 66, of which no fewer than 40 are in or around Great Yarmouth and Gorleston, and therefore only just beyond the Suffolk boundary. (Indeed, Gorleston did not become part of Norfolk until 1914.)

15. *Bradbourne, Larkfield, Kent : west front*

depended upon the use of a wooden centering. As soon as the key, or central brick, was placed in position, assuming, of course, that the abutments – the portions of supporting wall – were sufficiently strong, the centering could be safely removed. In the least refined examples all the wedge-shaped bricks were identical; and in the case of purpose-made bricks the arch joints are of the same thickness as those of the rest of the wall. But a much better effect is obtained if the joints between the bricks forming the arch are thinner; and this meant using a finer brick, soft enough to be rubbed down on the site if necessary. Hence a feature which is frequently in evidence in the better buildings of this period: the window-heads are not only more finely jointed but of a different colour (generally redder) from the rest of the walling. In specially refined examples each brick – or, to be quite accurate, each pair of bricks to either side of the key – had to be produced separately. In such cases the whole arch would first be carefully set out on the drawing board so that the precise shape of each brick could be determined. Then, with a special toothed saw, every brick would be cut to the shape required, and rubbed down so as to achieve the finest possible joint. Today, if it were done at all, a piece of carborundum would be used, but in 1700 it would probably have been either another brick

30

16. *Bradbourne, Larkfield, Kent : south side, detail*

or a slab of York or similar stone. Rubbers were often rubbed smooth
on their surface as well as at their jointing edges.

Ornamentation in brickwork far more elaborate than shaped arches
was, however, sometimes required and, moreover, achieved. Ever since
the time of those wonderful Tudor chimney-stacks, raised decoration
had always been a feature of the most expensive English brickwork.
This did not necessarily mean that special bricks were needed. Raised
patterns could be produced by the simple expedient of laying some of
the ordinary bricks with a projection of about an inch. Under eaves or
at the base of a cornice the ornamental feature known as dentilation
(small rectangular blocks, resembling a row of teeth) could be obtained
by laying a course of headers with every alternate one projecting. Or
one course of bricks could be laid diagonally to produce a serrated
edge, with projecting points.

But between the closing years of the seventeenth century and the
middle of the eighteenth the most ambitious builders in brick deman-
ded much more than that. They wanted 'aprons' under the more important windows, and panels, sometimes sunk, sometimes projecting,
on walls and parapets. Features like egg-and-dart mouldings and Ionic
capitals and other such familiar items in the vocabulary of classical

31

architecture could be supplied with no great difficulty, but how about
a swag of fruit and flowers, or a Corinthian capital with all its acanthus
leaves, or even a group of Cupids? Much of this ornamentation had to
be carved *in situ*. The utmost care was needed. Wire-saws, files and
sometimes strips of copper were brought into service, and much gentle
abrasion was required to arrive at the final results. That they were
achieved is a tribute to the consummate skill of the best brickworkers
of this epoch. In the West Hall of the Victoria and Albert Museum in
London can be seen the sumptuous window-frame of a late seventeenth-
century house at Enfield which was pulled down a good many years
ago. It is a masterpiece of carved and gauged brickwork, incorporating
a quartet of large, handsome capitals, a pair of fine swags of fruit and
foliage, and two delightful *amorini*. At Bradbourne (*15, 16*), a Queen
Anne house at Larkfield near Maidstone, the variety and resource-
fulness of the ornamental brickwork is easily the most memorable

feature of the house. Elsewhere, as at Pallant House, Chichester (*17*), not only are the window-heads exquisitely gauged and provided with a carved emblem on every key-block, but, as at Bradbourne, cut back at their base in delicately recessed curves. On the parapet at Pallant House the heads of the sunk panels appear to have been 'gathered' like the pelmets of a set of curtains, a remarkable although by no means unique example of virtuosity in the handling of brick.

It is significant that Pallant House should be not a grand country house but a 'middling' house in a prosperous market town. The merchants and professional men who owned these 'middling' houses were both able and willing to pay for the choicest refinements, and it is this, more than any other single factor, which makes those small towns that are rich in Georgian brick architecture one of the great delights of England. And happily there are many of them; from Farnham (*18*), to Ampthill, from Newbury to Colchester, from Blandford to

19. *Bridge Street, Pershore, Worcestershire*

Bewdley, from Pershore (*19*) to Tenterden, the list could easily be extended tenfold. Hampshire is specially lucky, with Lymington, Fareham (the part north of West Street), Wickham, Alton, New Alresford, and several more besides. There never was a time in our history, before or since, when people were prepared to spend such a large proportion of their incomes on their houses, and happily a great many of these buildings survive. Owners of sixteenth- and seventeenth-century houses, sometimes timber-framed, were in the eighteenth century much given to having them refronted in dignified Georgian brick, which has also contributed greatly to our pleasure.

Very occasionally an entire Georgian front would be constructed of rubbed bricks, and at Chicheley Hall in the northern corner of Buckinghamshire this can even be seen on two fronts, the one with the entrance doorway (*20*, *21*) and the other overlooking the garden. Including the garden walls, which accounted for some 85,000 of them, nearly a million bricks were needed for this one house. In a region of excellent clays these joyous bricks, of a rich orange-red, were almost certainly made on the site. Formerly attributed to Archer, it is now known that the architect of Chicheley, built between 1719 and 1723, was Francis Smith of Warwick.

34

ABOVE 20. *Chicheley Hall, Buckinghamshire :
south front*

RIGHT 21. *Chicheley Hall, Buckinghamshire :
south-west corner*

Until the eighteenth century nearly all these brick buildings were red, and of course the majority continued to be so – I would say very fortunately, for hardly any of the many shades of red characteristic of old bricks are other than agreeable, and some are a delight. None the less, in some fashionable circles in the eighteenth century there was a strong reaction against red. 'The colour is fiery', complained the architect Isaac Ware in 1756 (in his *Complete Body of Architecture*), 'and . . . there is something harsh in the transition from red brick to stone; it seems altogether unnatural.' And, he rightly observed, most buildings 'of any expense' have stone at least for the dressings, to which brick, although there would probably be much more of it, should always play second fiddle. So, he argued, the nearer the bricks came to the colour of the stone the better. These precepts were followed at many (although at by no means all) of the Palladian houses which, where they are not red, are usually brown or a rather washed-out, dusty-looking yellow.

Although the range of brick colours was very much smaller than it is today, certain others were available in the eighteenth century, but, because of the high cost of transport, only in those districts where the appropriate clays could be dug locally. As I have observed elsewhere,[1] the term white when applied to bricks has, as with wines, a connotation of elegance rather than of exactitude. There are no white, unglazed bricks, and this is no cause for regret. But in order to make the sober-coloured bricks which the Palladians so much preferred, it was necessary, as noted earlier, to find clay with a good deal of lime in its composition. In England such clays principally occur in the Gault and in the Jurassic and Pleistocene clays to either side of it, all of which formations belong only to the south-eastern half of the country. They were, however, extensively used in and around Ipswich, over large parts of Cambridgeshire, the Isle of Ely, the Soke of Peterborough, Huntingdonshire and Bedfordshire; also in the Maidstone district and at certain places on the South coast.

Brown bricks were specially characteristic of the Thames Valley; in London itself the reticent yellow-brown 'stocks' were much preferred to red through most of the eighteenth century and much of the nineteenth, too (*22*). There was also a darker brown which can frequently be seen in the Vale of York. But the most elegant non-reds of the Georgian age are without a doubt the silver-greys of south Oxford-

[1] See *The Pattern of English Building* (1972), p. 234.

shire, Berkshire, parts of Hampshire and to a small extent elsewhere. Lime in the clay is again the essential factor. Some of these bricks became lightly vitrified in the making, but a good many did not. If the necessary lime were lacking, a thin grey 'skin' could be produced by adding salt to the sand before firing. A sure sign of the special esteem which these grey bricks enjoyed in the Georgian period is that one sometimes finds a house that is red at the back and sides and wholly grey in front, as at Eastwood House, Wickham (*23*).

The juxtaposition of bricks of more than one colour occurs in various ways throughout the eighteenth century. Reference has already been made to the deeper reds of gauged window-heads; this may extend to the entire architecture of the window, and perhaps to the apron below. A colour refinement in evidence on the front at Bradbourne (*15*) is the introduction of bricks of a paler tone down the centre of each of the eight pilasters, whereas the central window, by contrast, is framed within a velvet 'curtain' of a darker red than the rest. But the commonest type of Georgian polychromy is also, appropriately enough, the

23. *Eastwood House, Wickham, Hampshire*

simplest: the all-over chequer pattern, the headers being blue-grey and the stretchers red or pink. There are places in south-eastern England, and especially in the Kentish Weald, where almost every Georgian building down to the most modest has its front enlivened by this reticent but most effective diaper, so easy to produce in Flemish bond but impossible in English. At The Moot, Downton (*24*), externally a specially delightful example of a 'middling' house of about 1700, the central projection, apart from the limestone dressings and the white wood-framed pediment, is all red brick, whereas the flanking walls are gently diapered. Cottages at Cuxham near Watlington (*25*) have diapered side-walls but along the front the silver-greys are introduced as horizontal bands.

It was not until the eighteenth century that brick began at last to be extensively employed for small houses. The farm labourer up to 1700 would have been even less likely to inhabit a brick house than a stone one, for stone might be lying around waiting to be used, whereas bricks always had to be made by someone who understood how to do

38

24. *The Moot, Downton, Wiltshire*

25. *Cuttmill Cottage, Cuxham, Oxfordshire*

it. The humbler people used brick, as has already been observed, at first just for chimney-shafts, as a precaution against fire. Only in a few areas, such as Fenland and Breckland, where wood had become scarce by the beginning of the seventeenth century and where, apart perhaps from flint, there was no available stone, was brick used for cottages under the first two Stuarts. But in Georgian times brick became normal for even the humblest dwellings over large parts of England. It was only the incidence of the brick tax, which was first imposed in 1784, increased in 1794 and again in 1803, and not finally repealed until 1850, that checked for a while the use of this material for cottages. It is largely because of the brick tax that weather-boarded cottages in the South-East – which is where most of them are – will nearly always be found to date from the late eighteenth or first half of the nineteenth centuries.

Another effect of the brick tax was the strong incentive which was given after 1784 to the use of brick-tiles, which were not subject to it. I suppose that most people in England have never seen a brick-tile and have little or no idea what it is, while many others will have seen plenty of them without realizing it. And this is exactly what was intended: the brick-tile was designed to deceive. The face looks exactly like a brick, but the thickness at the base may only be $\frac{1}{4}$ in. Attached to it is a flange, which projects upwards and slightly backwards (cf. p. 75). Although never seen, this is indispensable, for in it is the hole for the nail upon which the brick-tile is suspended.

Brick-tiles were in use before the imposition of the tax, but only in very small numbers. The earliest that has so far been identified is on the wall of the Malthouse at Westcott in Surrey, which carries the date 1724 (61).[1] The brick-tile which is dated is in itself a great rarity. Nor is much known about the reasons why they were first made. It seems likely, however, that their original purpose was to encase timber-framed houses, in order to make them both more fireproof and more fashionable. The usual practice was to attach battens or boards to the oak studs of the earlier house and to nail on the brick-tiles (either hung dry or bedded in mortar), as with tile-hanging. Another method was to render the whole wall externally and to bed the brick-tiles into the plaster: this would have been more feasible where the original wall, as was sometimes the case, was of rough stone, pebbles or brick.

To apply a veneer of brick-tiles to a stone or brick wall seems at first very curious; but there were several motives for it. The stone may have proved porous or worn badly. It may, again, have seemed insufficiently urbane, as for example with flint or beach-cobbles; there are a number of instances of these being later masked by brick-tiles at Brighton when in the early nineteenth century it became a centre of fashion. To be up-to-date was a constant preoccupation in the South-East, which is virtually the only part of the country in which brick-tiles were made or used. At Nunwell near Brading in the Isle of Wight the east wing, built in 1716 of the local stone, was later covered with brick-tiles to make it look more 'modern'. At Salisbury No. 47 Winchester Street is a brick house of the seventeenth century, converted to appear Georgian by the addition of a brick-tile facing. At this house the nails were actually driven straight into the earlier bricks. At Hythe there is a house which was once red but which, thanks to the addition in the early years of the nineteenth century of an overcoat of brick-tiles, became yellowish; this, it may be supposed, is another example of the fashionable reaction against red at this time, referred to earlier. Among the big country houses, Chevening in Kent and Althorp in Northamptonshire are often

[1] We owe this discovery to Miss Joan Harding, F.S.A., to whom grateful acknowledgment is made.

cited in connection with the masking of red brick. At Chevening the tiles were made to the client's own specification – intended to be fireproof – and were notably unpleasing; their complete removal in 1970 is one of the reasons why that house now looks so much more attractive than at any time since 1786. At Althorp the tiles were attached to wooden laths, which decayed and in recent years have had to be entirely renewed: most of the old tiles were able to be used again.

When they were first introduced, brick-tiles were no cheaper than bricks; they required less clay but were more trouble to make. Nor were any efforts spared: the best houses even have brick-tile rubbers for their window-heads, all meticulously jointed. The practical advantage of brick-tiles was that they were lighter. But when it was found that they were not subject to the brick tax, they were at once very much in demand, even for large houses like Belmont Park near Faversham, built for the first Lord Harris by Samuel Wyatt in 1792. Here pale yellow brick-tiles were employed throughout for the facing material. The only surprise is that this demand was still confined to the South and South-East, where, mysteriously, they were usually known as 'mathematical' tiles. They can be found at both Salisbury and Winchester, while Sussex and Kent towns like Lewes, Rye, Hythe, Tenterden (26) and Canterbury can still show a good many examples. To detect them one should look at the windows, which will usually be nearly flush with

26. *Tenterden, Kent*

the walls, and, whenever the site allows, at the angles, which are often masked by strips of wood. Nowadays, too, it is not unusual to see surface irregularities caused by a brick-tile having here and there slipped out of position; this is due to some of the nails by which they were secured having rusted and decayed. Repairs are practically impossible without taking down the entire wall of tiles.

A special development in and around Brighton was the glazed brick-tile, which was usually black. This was produced to afford protection against a salt-laden atmosphere. No better example can be cited than Brighton's Royal Crescent (1799–1807), which, underneath its veneer of black-glazed tiles, is of red brick. These tiles are rightly pointed with a very light-coloured mortar, and are all laid in header bond.

Despite the tax, however, brick was being used in England during the first half of the nineteenth century to a quite unprecedented extent. Before Victoria ascended the throne there were already enormous dockside warehouses and many large factories built entirely of brick, which was also employed extensively in the construction of the canals, many miles of which required brick linings in order to render them waterproof. As for Regency houses, many more are of brick than might at first appear. The reason is that this was the great age of stucco, an economical substitute for stone at a time when stone was without question the most socially desirable material. The Englishman's aspiration towards stone, or at least to a surface finish resembling stone, was greatly assisted by the invention of a number of patent external renderings: Liardet's cement, much used by the Adam brothers, from 1773; Parker's Roman cement from 1796; Dehl's mastic from 1815; Hamelin's mastic from 1817; Portland cement from 1824. Nash and his contemporaries laid on Parker's cement, one might say, by the acre; a well-known tag of the time summed it up thus:

Augustus at Rome was for building renowned,
For of marble he left what of brick he had found:
But isn't our Nash, too, a very great master?
He finds us all brick and he leaves us all plaster!

Eventually, however, the greater strength and durability of Portland cement pushed all the others off the market, which aesthetically was a pity, as Portland cement as a facing material is not visually pleasing.

43

27. Bengeo Hall, Hertford : west wing

Few people, I imagine, will have heard of Hitch bricks: they are now collectors' pieces. Yet they also belong to this period; it was in 1828 that Caleb Hitch, a brickmaker of Ware in Hertfordshire, was granted a patent for the production of large interlocking bricks of most unusual shapes. A wall of Hitch bricks – and the most striking surviving example is the west wing of Bengeo Hall, just north of Hertford (27) – looks very like one erected of rat-trap bond (in which standard-sized bricks are laid on edge), but behind the face it is very different. The distinguishing characteristic of Hitch bricks was their numerous cavities, which, as their inventor pointed out, meant less weight, less mortar and lower costs. Unfortunately, however, stability could only be obtained, or so Caleb Hitch believed, by the introduction at intervals of special bricks of complicated form, which had to be made in beechwood moulds designed for the purpose. It is said that to turn a corner in a 9-in wall in Hitch bricks required seven different shapes, so it is not surprising that builders were generally unresponsive. These bricks are only to be found in the immediate vicinity of Ware, and, although very ingenious, were killed by over-complication. Including bricks for coping, cresting and buttressing, no fewer than thirty-two different types were produced.[1]

After the abolition of the brick tax in 1850, which was a year before the repeal of the still more undesirable tax on windows, the demand for bricks quickly rose to unprecedented heights. Stucco now went out of favour, and partly (remember the date) for moral reasons; because it was intended to be mistaken for stone, and therefore to deceive – and of this there can be no question: every Regency and early Victorian stuccoed house was originally covered with a mesh of punctiliously incised lines meant to suggest the courses between the blocks – it was regarded as a dishonest material, and therefore became taboo. Thus did brick again come into its own.

It did so at a time of brilliant mechanical inventiveness, and it was not long before mechanization entered into the manufacture of bricks. Machines were invented for drying the clay by means of steam or hot air, and also for grinding, which enabled the harder but less plastic carbonaceous shales of the North Midlands and the North to be

[1] For further information on Hitch bricks, see the paper by Gordon E. Moodey published by the East Herts Archaeological Society, 1971. I am also much indebted to Mr Christopher Savory of Bengeo Hall for information with regard to these.

brought for the first time into the service of the brickmaker. In 1858 the invention of the Hoffman kiln rendered it possible for the coal fires to be kept burning night and day: only in slack periods, or for repairs, are they allowed to go out. The Hoffman kiln is shaped like an elongated circle, with a number of openings or 'ports'. As the heat travels round, it is used to dry the 'green' bricks awaiting firing. After 1858 most bricks were made by machinery in metal moulds, either in power-operated, belt-driven presses, or by squeezing a band of prepared clay through a mill and along rollers to a cutting table, upon which it was sliced into the sizes required by vertical wires suspended from a mechanically operated frame. Pressed bricks and wire-cuts have been the stock-in-trade of the brick merchant for the last hundred years. And in a large Hoffman kiln as many as 40,000 might be fired at a time. It was not long before the enterprising Edward Gripper secured a contract for the exclusive use of Hoffman kilns in the Nottingham area. The outcome was Gripper's Patent Bricks, which, although they were expensive, Scott insisted on using in London in 1865–71 for the St Pancras Hotel (*28*).

Apart from a substantial reduction in costs, the great virtue of these mechanical processes was that they made possible the attainment of absolute uniformity. Where the brickwork was to be covered with plaster or some other finish, as in nearly all internal work, the convenience was obvious. One could now be sure that every brick would be virtually identical in both colour and texture, precisely so in size, and perfectly true. Aesthetically, of course, this was often no advantage at all, but it is fair to add that it could be. For a building such as the chimney-stack of the Western Pumping Station in Pimlico, London (*29*), uniform bricks were clearly desirable. This imposing structure, which dates from 1875, is in 'white' (that is, pale yellow) brick, and I never pass it on the way into Victoria Station by train without a sensation of pleasure. Uniformity in brickwork is seen at its best where the same motif is many times reiterated. Another specially good London example is the long wall of the goods station at St Pancras.[1]

For engineering work, also, there was everything to be said for

---

[1] This is illustrated in Jack Simmons's *St. Pancras Station* (1968), plate 41. Professor Simmons draws particular attention to the perfect regularity of the bricks and to the evenness of the pointing. These excellent machine-made bricks, of a slightly orange-red, came from Leicestershire, and possibly from Swannington.

28. *Former hotel, St Pancras, London : from south-west*

uniformity. Specially strong bricks were now made for the engineers. Nor are all these bricks unpleasant to look at: 'Staffordshire blues', which are made from the very tough carbonaceous clays of southern Staffordshire and fired at a very high temperature (up to 1200 °C), are not only particularly suitable for industrial purposes because of their strength, hardness and ability to resist damp, but can look rather good. Their colour is always more grey than blue, but varies from slate-grey through blue-grey (the most familiar) to a lustrous dark purple-grey. They are sufficiently pleasing to have been selected from time to time for domestic buildings, where great strength is not a requirement. It has, however, to be admitted that many of the bricks made from the shales of the Coal Measures are among the ugliest we have. This is mainly due to their colours, among which the hot, dense reds of central Lancashire are especially harsh on the eyes. ('Accrington bloods' are notorious in this respect.) But the textures of these bricks, especially when glazed, are very insensitive too, while, considered aesthetically, sizes also changed for the worse. Here the culprit was originally the brick tax. Since the duty was levied on every thousand bricks, there was a strong incentive to increase the sizes. The thickness of bricks rose to 3 in and sometimes even to $3\frac{1}{4}$ in, and when machines were introduced these ungainly dimensions were often unfortunately maintained in the Midlands and in the North.[1]

The dominant building material of Victorian England was undoubtedly brick. With the rapid increase in population – England and Wales had about 15 million inhabitants at the Queen's accession and some $32\frac{1}{2}$ millions at her death – there was in fact a greater use of stone, but it was as nothing compared with the immense increase in the employment of brick. For the poor as for the rich, brick now became the normal material for housing, even in some areas where stone was locally available. Railway towns like Derby, Crewe and Swindon, none of which is far from good building stone, were constructed almost

[1] The brick tax (1784) was responsible for the production, for a few years only, of much larger bricks than these. In his *Building Materials* (1972), Kenneth Hudson describes the double-size bricks made in Sir Joseph Wilkes's brickyard at Measham in Leicestershire and given a local soubriquet, 'Wilkes's Gobs'. Examples can still be seen at Measham and nearby at Ashby-de-la-Zouch. When the duty was increased (for the second time) in 1803, bricks of more than 150 cu in ($10 \times 5 \times 3$ in) had to pay double, which effectively killed these outsize products. For these and other examples of very large bricks, see also John Woodforde, *Bricks to Build a House* (1976), pp. 70-1.

wholly of brick, and of very unattractive brick too; there can be no doubt whatever that the first consideration was cheapness. Industrial buildings of all kinds, factories and breweries and mills, were now usually built of brick, and so, with increasing frequency, were such buildings as theatres, enormous hotels like the Grand at Scarborough (by Cuthbert Brodrick, 1867: of yellow and red brick) or St Pancras in London (mentioned above) and great public buildings such as the Victoria Law Courts in Birmingham (by Sir Aston Webb and Ingress Bell, 1887–91). Alfred Waterhouse was also much addicted to terra-cotta, and liked a hard red brick of peculiar ferocity, as for the Prudential building in High Holborn, London (mainly 1899–1906). A good many lesser architects shared this strange taste. 'It is faced with that cursed imperishable red Victorian brick, which is such crushing proof of technical proficiency and aesthetic dumbness' is how Sir Nikolaus Pevsner describes the Shire Hall at Durham of 1897–8, by Henry Barnes and F. E. Coates. As for the Market Hall at Ludlow by Harry Cheers of Twickenham (1887), a horrific red blot on that gentle and otherwise beautiful town, Sir Nikolaus again has *le mot juste*: 'Ludlow's bad luck.' These Victorian bricks have manifested an almost frightening durability, and it is a chastening thought that some are still likely to be seen three, and perhaps five, hundred years hence.

Brick, as has already been indicated, was the normal material of the railway builders. In addition to innumerable stations, train-sheds, signal-boxes, level-crossing keepers' cottages and the many other buildings which a railway demands, countless millions of bricks were used to line cuttings and tunnels. Most spectacular of all were the bridges and viaducts. Some of Brunel's brick bridges on the Great Western are world-famous for the audacity of their spans and for the gentleness of their curvature; indeed, the one which crosses the Thames at Maidenhead, erected in 1837–8 and later widened, is said to lead the world in both these respects. The twin arches are each 128 ft wide and rise only 24 ft. Brunel's Wharncliffe Viaduct at Hanwell has a truly Roman grandeur, yet visually the Ouse Viaduct at Balcombe in Sussex is still more memorable (*30*). Dating from 1839–41, this was the work of David Mocatta, the architect, and John Urpeth Rastrick, the engineer of the London to Brighton line. The length is 1,476 ft and at the centre it is close on 100 ft high. The special feature is that the huge tapering piers of the thirty-seven brick arches, each with a span of 30 ft,

30. *Ouse Valley Railway Viaduct, Balcombe, Sussex*

are also themselves pierced: the long narrow openings are arched at the top and, invertedly, at the base too (*31*). The balustrade is of Caen stone, and so are the four little classical pavilions, purely ornamental in intention, at each end. For the Great Northern Railway, in 1850, Thomas Brassey, Lewis Cubitt's contractor, built the Digswell Viaduct near Welwyn. This is plainer, but still longer (1,560 ft, with forty arches) and took 13 million bricks. There are of course many more of these railway viaducts; sometimes they are great embellishments to the landscape. The finest, no doubt, are in stone; the ugliest, the Forth Bridge excepted, in iron; the flimsiest-looking (and none now survives) in timber; the most numerous in brick.

In contrast to the Netherlands, northern Germany, parts of Italy and elsewhere, brick, except in Essex, a county notably deficient in stone, was not much used for English church-building in the Middle Ages; but later Stuart and Georgian churches outside London are more likely to be of brick than of stone, simply because it was cheaper. (And even in the City of London itself the fabrics were all of brick: only the steeples and the parts which showed were sometimes faced with Portland stone.) It is because they are built of brick that the exteriors of

most Georgian churches, although always well proportioned, are usually decidedly plain. Brick was also the usual material for churches after the Napoleonic wars. Nearly two hundred went up between 1820 and 1850 in what are now mostly the inner suburbs of London; they were built of stock bricks, with the stone dressings usually pared down to the minimum – and very poverty-stricken many of them look. Only a few of these churches were stuccoed. The early Victorians, on the other hand, despite a few notable exceptions like J. Wild's Christ Church, Streatham (1842), tended to regard brick as a mean material inappropriate to a building consecrated to the worship of God, and reverted to stone whenever resources permitted. But as the century advanced economics got the better of such scruples, and all over the country the later Victorian churches will often be found to be of brick. Among many striking examples, special mention may be made of St Augustine, Kilburn (1870–80), the leading example in London of the work of J. L. Pearson, not for the beauty of its brickwork but for its audacity; the entire church is brick-vaulted, with internal brick buttresses which owe something to the cathedral of Albi, the great mediaeval brick cathedral of southern France. In those same years, and drawing inspiration from the same source, G. F. Bodley built, just to the north-west of Manchester, St Augustine, Pendlebury (1871–4), which Pevsner considers to be 'one of the most moving of all Victorian churches', with an interior 'of breathtaking majesty and purity'. By 1900 most of our church architects were employing brick for new churches almost as a matter of course, for unless there was a patron, rich and generous, stone was usually too expensive. Some architects, such as Norman Shaw and Lutyens, whose work was usually domestic or, later, official, may even have preferred to use brick for their churches. St Martin, New Knebworth (32), is a delightful example by Lutyens, built in 1914. The most ambitious example of Victorian church building in brick was also the last: Westminster Cathedral by J. F. Bentley (1895–1903). For this $12\frac{1}{2}$ million bricks were required, most of which came from the Oxford Clay, where, as we shall see (p. 57), brickmaking was still a new industry. In the Sienese manner, the external brickwork is liberally interspersed with horizontal bands of Portland stone, specially prominent on the lofty campanile, which soars to 273 ft. Functionally these stripes are very unfortunate, for whenever it rains lime is washed out of the stone on to the surface of the bricks, with

31. *Ouse Valley Railway Viaduct, Balcombe, Sussex:*
view through piers

32. *St Martin, New Knebworth, Hertfordshire : west front*

chemical effects which are beginning to become a matter of serious concern. If internally the brickwork looks rough (as it does), this is because the architect's intention was that the entire surface of the cathedral should ultimately be clothed with marbles and mosaics.

About 1850 polychrome surface patterns, which apart from the reticent diapers of the Georgian period had not been seen in English brickwork since the time of the Tudors, suddenly reappeared. These are specially associated with Butterfield, but Street and some of the lesser Victorian architects indulged in them with almost equal zest. Why, one asks, is Tudor polychromy so agreeable and Victorian usually very much the reverse? The reason is undoubtedly that, when machine-pressed bricks were used, the pattern could be executed with relentless efficiency and without even the slightest variation from diamond to diamond. Ruskin, who with his devotion to Italian Gothic architecture was enthusiastic about polychromatic brickwork, nevertheless had no illusions about what its character should be. 'Colour', he says in *The Seven Lamps of Architecture*, 'to be perfect, *must* have a soft outline and a simple one.' This may perhaps be taken as implying that where the lines are simple they need not be soft, a point well illustrated by a tall Victorian brick building, formerly a granary, in Queen Charlotte Street, Bristol (*33*), which was obviously inspired by Italian Romanesque architecture (although the Ghibelline battlements are somewhat later!). Here white bricks have been used for horizontal banding at widely spaced intervals, and, alternately with pink, for the voussoirs of the arches, some of which are also outlined in black. The outcome is not a harlequinade but a welcome addition of liveliness to a building so large that reliance upon a single colour might well have proved monotonous.

Their attraction to polychromy, allied to their love of surface ornamentation, prompted the Victorians to develop a lively interest in the manufacture of terracotta. 'Terracotta', we read in what at the time of writing is the latest volume of the monumental *Survey of London*, 'became the hallmark of the South Kensington style'. The products ranged from plain, though lightly glazed, substitutes for facing bricks, through small (and sometimes not so small) ornamental mould-made plaques (usually deep red) embodying strapwork, cartouches, swags of fruit and flowers, *amorini* and so on, for incorporation into the brickwork of many a domestic façade, to the most ambitious substitutes for sculpture. The place of provenance was generally Staffordshire. The most remarkable example is Waterhouse's Natural History Museum, the brick front of which, at considerable additional cost, was entirely faced with terracotta, principally buff but with a certain amount of blue-grey for contrast. With a century's accumulation of soot the effect of contrast was all but lost and this had become one of the most disagreeable surfaces to be seen anywhere. But one of the advantages of terracotta, and one specially emphasized by Waterhouse, is that it can be cleaned very easily; the cleaning, therefore, in 1974 was much overdue. It came as a revelation. It is not too much to say that the Natural History Museum, always architecturally impressive, is now also, visually, one of the most enjoyable Victorian buildings in London.

The most significant change that has taken place in the story of English brickmaking during the last hundred years has been the

exploitation of the immense bed of Oxford Clay (so called), which occupies most of the area between the limestone belt and, at its southern end, the Chilterns. This dates only from 1880. Today nearly half the total number of bricks produced in England are from this Jurassic clay, which stretches from Oxfordshire to Lincolnshire; and to the south and east of Bedford and at Fletton and Orton, south of Peterborough, huge clay pits up to 40 ft deep, often now filled with water, and flanked by clusters of extremely tall chimneys, have wrought havoc with the countryside. The sizes and textures of these bricks were from the outset less disagreeable than those made from the Coal Measures shales, but the colours, instead of being too dense, were very liable to be too pale. Indeed, half a century ago Fletton was a byword for an anaemic kind of machine-pressed brick whose only virtue was its cheapness; but these were 'commons', in which appearance was of no concern. Fletton facing bricks, which are either faced with sand or machine textured, are visually more acceptable.

Yet the market for high-quality hand-moulded bricks never entirely disappeared, even during the most philistine phase of Victorianism. Architects such as Eden Nesfield, Norman Shaw – notably at Leyswood near Groombridge, an influential Sussex house built in 1869 but now mostly demolished – and Basil Champneys used such bricks whenever they felt that their clients could afford them. Champneys was responsible for notably good work from 1875 onwards at Newnham College, Cambridge (34, 35), where the carved brick ornamentation is as accomplished as any in the country. The fine joints here should be noticed: they run along and rise through the carving. Aesthetically this is a consideration which should not be overlooked, for thereby it can be seen that the ornamental enrichment is not just an afterthought but an integral part of the building.

By the end of the century the architects of the next generation, Edwin Lutyens, Guy Dawber, Detmar Blow and others, were requiring hand-moulded bricks of fine quality in ever-increasing numbers. For these bricks it is necessary to have clay with plenty of plasticity, which is coated with sand before being thrown into the mould. Because of its dampness the bricks may shrink considerably, and unevenly, during the process of drying and firing, which may present problems. But it is precisely for these irregularities of shape and variations in texture and colour, qualities in which the machine-made products were

so deficient, that the hand-made bricks were especially valued. Their principal use was for facing. An easy way of producing pleasing and interesting colour variations was by sprinkling differently coloured sands over the moulds. There was also a reversion to narrower bricks. Lutyens, who has a strong claim to be regarded as the greatest English architect of the last hundred years, showed his mastery and unending inventiveness in the use of hand-made bricks; he often liked them to be no thicker than 2 in, with wide and sometimes recessed mortar joints. He also obtained still richer effects of texture by the incorporation into his facing walls – for instance, for the arch over a door – of tiles laid on end, as at The Deanery, Sonning (*36*). Of course these bricks were more expensive, but there is never any hope of seeing fine architecture if the overriding consideration is cutting costs to the minimum. Lutyens was fortunate, certainly, in often being employed by clients with very long purses.

Hand-moulded bricks are still made, but since the cost may be three times as much as the machine products they do not find it easy to com-

pete. Nevertheless, in his well-informed book *Bricks to Build a House* (1976), Mr John Woodforde is able to assure us that the rate of closure of small firms producing fine quality hand-made bricks has lately slowed down, and that a few closed works of this kind have even managed to reopen. He suggests that this is because the price of the bricks is now such a relatively small part of the total cost of building a house. Of Britain's total annual output of approximately 7,500 million bricks, about 150 million, or 2 per cent, is now moulded by hand. To come upon such bricks is invariably a pleasure. In recent years an outstanding example is Kings Walden Bury in Hertfordshire, a country house of classical inspiration completed in 1971. Special hand-made bricks measuring $9\frac{3}{4} \times 4\frac{3}{4} \times 2$ in were commissioned by the architects, Raymond Erith and Quinlan Terry, from the brickworks at Bulmer Tye near Sudbury, Suffolk.

After 1930 an important influence on English brick buildings was the Dutch architect W. M. Dudok, whose Town Hall at Hilversum, completed in that year, made a great impression well beyond the con-

fines of Holland. This building is memorable not only for its cubic, geometrical forms culminating in a lofty and striking tower and for the gracious lawns, flowers and formal pools which provide the perfect setting, but also for its brickwork. It is built of thin machine-made biscuit-coloured bricks laid in quite elaborate bonds, with recessed joints over the entire surface. Occasionally turquoise-blue glazed bricks add colourful accents. The Dudok influence is evident in such English buildings as Francis Lorne's St Dunstan's at Rottingdean (which is of yellow brick) and Herbert Rowse's Philharmonic Hall in Liverpool (37), both of 1937-9, and it even spread to utility buildings like pit-head baths and to some of the excellent stations erected at that time for the London Underground. Many cinemas also show the influence, while among brick churches a good example is St Nicholas at Burnage (38), a south-eastern suburb of Manchester, built in 1931-2 by Welch, Cachemaille-Day and Lander.

OPPOSITE 36. *The Deanery, Sonning, Berkshire : archway*

RIGHT 37. *Philharmonic Hall, Hope Street, Liverpool : front*

BELOW 38. *St Nicholas, Burnage, Manchester : porch*

Machine-made bricks are usually much better-looking today than they were a century ago. A visit to the Building Centre in London will reveal that a wide choice of colours is now available. It is indeed in the field of colour that the greatest advances have been made during the present century. All the large firms now have their laboratories, and there is a far better, more scientific understanding of the chemical composition of the various types of clay and shale at the disposal of the brickmakers, and also of what can be achieved in the course of firing; easy transport means that clays from different regions can now be blended, and other colouring agents introduced. The outcome of all this research has been the production of manufactured bricks in an astonishingly broad range of colours, including some which show variations across the face of each individual brick. The bricklayer needs himself to be something of an artist to handle to the best advantage bricks such as these.

Hardly less notable is the variety of textures which can now be offered, through the skilful addition of sand and other agents. They range from smooth to rock-faced, and combed, creased, stippled, coarse-dragged (vertical or horizontal), grit-particled and semi-vitreous are the names of some of the other textures available. Not all, needless to say, are equally pleasing. Some of the current processes, such as the application, before firing, of lightly incised striations, straight or wavy (and only on one side and at one end of each brick), to produce what is called 'a rustic face', are decidedly tricky; yet it is undeniable that, where on account of the cost hand-moulded, sand-faced bricks are ruled out, these artificially textured bricks are often a good second best.

Nowadays bricks are often used non-structurally as panelling between the members of steel or reinforced concrete buildings. This has encouraged architects and builders to experiment with elaborate textures and honeycombed brickwork, especially where such panel walls screen car parks. On the other hand, the widespread use of cavity-wall construction both with structural frames and in the load-bearing walls of small houses led to the dull uniformity of stretcher bond taking the place of the much more varied and interesting bonding of former days.

Bricks are not always made from clay or shale. Today's builder can use calcium silicate (sand-lime) bricks, which are made by blending silica sand, crushed stone, siliceous gravel, or a mixture of these, with hydrated lime and, if desired, a colouring agent as well. The final colour will depend on what sand or aggregate has been used in the process of manufacture. Usually, however, the colours of calcium silicate bricks are light: pale pink, cream and off-white, as a general rule. They do not vary much from one brick to another, and this of course is often an advantage. They are also relatively inexpensive.

They are not, however, suitable for paving, for which some of the tougher clay and shale bricks are now in demand. These can not only look delightful but are for this purpose both practical and durable. In busy situations it will probably be desirable to lay them over a concrete base or at least to bed them in mortar, but elsewhere a base of well consolidated earth will usually suffice. In public places paving laid in unjointed rings provides an ideal 'frame' for a tree, with the important additional advantage that as the tree grows the inner ring or rings can be removed. Herring-bone paving offers a pleasing variation which should nevertheless not be indulged too often.[1]

Where on new housing estates brick is still the principal facing material, as, quite rightly, it often is, one may find nowadays that the architects have gone to some trouble to produce pleasing colours and acceptable textures, and the public itself would now seem to be more aware of their value. What is also certain is that the building materials most typical of the twentieth century, concrete, steel and glass, have by no means ousted brick. For smaller buildings, and for houses in particular, this still remains, over nearly the whole of England, the most human building material and often the best.

No consideration of brickwork would be complete which failed to take into account the choice of mortar and how it has been handled, for the beauty of a building can be enhanced or quite seriously compromised by right or wrong practices in this respect. The basis of mortar is coarse sand, which used always to be mixed with slaked lime, the colour being determined by the choice of sand or, sometimes, of the hard crushed stone which could be used as a substitute for it. During the last hundred years or so, lime has been superseded by Portland cement, which is tougher and easier to use but visually less attractive, as its

---

[1] For paving and other contemporary uses of brick, the reader is referred to the very useful and well-illustrated series of technical studies and information sheets by Cecil C. Handisyde, published in *The Architects' Journal* at various dates in 1975 and 1976, beginning on 7 May 1975, under the general title 'Hard Landscape in Brick'.

natural colour is a cold grey. Portland cement mortar can however be improved by the addition of various colouring agents, of which the oxides of iron are the most important.

Regarding the colour of mortar, there is one aesthetic principle which is always valid: it should be lighter in tone than the bricks. In the Victorian period there was a fashion for black mortar, which was produced by mixing Portland cement with crushed clinkers or ashes; many buildings have been marred by this horrible concoction. On the other hand, an excessively light tone is also to be avoided because, as with very dark mortar, the effect is to over-emphasize the individual bricks at the expense of the whole wall (see 65), with inevitable loss of scale and dignity. Mortar, in fact, although it should always be 'part of the picture', should be reticent and not draw attention to itself. Illustrations 43 and 44 (pp. 69 and 70) point the contrast immediately.

The width of the mortar courses has a very important part to play in the visual impact of any brick – or indeed stone – building. In mediaeval and Tudor times mortar courses were irregular but had to be comparatively wide – seldom less than half an inch and sometimes double as much – because so many of the bricks were far from true when removed from the kiln after firing. So in these buildings the mortar courses always figure prominently (see 2). But in the seventeenth century, with the advent of classical architecture and the growing skill of the brickmakers, brick dimensions became more regular, and the width of the mortar courses could now be reduced (see 18). And when cut and rubbed bricks were used, the aim was to suppress the joints still more; very thin joints were considered a desirable refinement, which in this type of brickwork they certainly were (see 72). Here and there, feeling that ordinary lime mortar was too coarse, they used instead what was known as lime putty (see 82). This was chalk, boiled with water into a creamy-white liquid and passed through a closely meshed sieve, after which it was allowed to settle for several days. Then some very fine, specially selected sand was washed through the sieve, and the two were carefully blended.

Before the advent of machine-made bricks, the acme of this concern with very thin joints as a mark of refinement was reached in the eighteenth century with what was known as 'tuck' pointing. The first step was to produce, by the addition of carefully selected sand and perhaps an oxide, a mortar as close as possible in colour to that of the bricks

64

themselves. This was applied flush with the brickface, and immediately, before it had had time to dry, a groove $\frac{1}{8}$ in deep and between $\frac{1}{8}$ in and $\frac{1}{4}$ in wide was scored along the centre of each joint. Into this groove was 'tucked' a band of white chalk-lime putty, usually with a slight projection (see *84*). After careful trimming, an effect of super-fine jointing was indeed produced, as can often be seen in those parts of London which were fashionable in the reign of George III. But this laborious process was always expensive, and aesthetically may be felt hardly to justify all the trouble involved.

With the advent of machine-made bricks, still finer joints presented no problem. Not only was every brick identical and undeviatingly regular; in addition, bricks were made with 'frogs' on each side: that is to say, with shallow indentations into which additional mortar could be pressed, thus making it possible to reduce the joints at the face to $\frac{1}{4}$ in or even less. Where very thin joints are required, the frog (which also helps to reduce weight) is an excellent idea. Hand-made bricks sometimes have it, but on one side only, in which case they are laid with the frog uppermost.

But with the more roughly textured bricks thin mortar joints do not look well, nor indeed are they practicable if the arrises of the bricks are a little irregular. Lutyens, of course, knew this very well, and his mortar joints will usually be found to be $\frac{3}{8}$ in thick even when, as already mentioned, the thickness of his bricks was only 2 in.

Only a little less important than the nature of the mortar itself is the manner in which it is applied. There are many kinds of joints that can be employed when the mortar is $\frac{3}{8}$ in or more broad: the flush or flat joint, the recessed or sunk joint, the struck or weather joint (with an inclined face, to throw off the rain) and even the projecting joint – but this is only used if a key is required for some kind of rendering. Recessed joints give interesting shadows and look well with rough-surfaced, richly textured bricks, but otherwise flush joints are aesthetically the best (see *46*); great care must be taken not to splodge the mortar over the edges of the bricks, which is always the mark of an indifferent or careless craftsman, as can be seen all too well in the repairs to the curved wall at Beverley (*48*).

Now and again one is likely to see new brickwork marred by a white efflorescence on the surface. This is due to the clay having in its composition an excess of salt (calcium or magnesium sulphate). It is always more likely to occur if the bricks are allowed to get very wet during the period of construction. In mild cases this white deposit will gradually disappear after a few years, and the application of a mild solution of acetic acid may hasten the process; but if the salts are present in considerable quantities it can be very disfiguring. One has therefore to be absolutely sure that the right clay is used at the brickmaking stage.

Two

Glossary

ACCRINGTON BRICKS: hard, smooth, deep-red pressed bricks made of shale from the Coal Measures near Accrington in East Lancashire; widely used for engineering and industrial purposes and also for many other building types in the late 19th and early 20th centuries. One of the trade names 'Nori' is 'iron' spelled backwards and indicates the character of the brick.

AIR BRICK: a brick pierced to provide for ventilation.

AMERICAN BOND: a term used in the United States for ENGLISH GARDEN-WALL BOND (q.v., under BONDING).

APRON: a projecting panel below a window sill, sometimes ornamented; a popular embellishment in the 18th century.

ARRIS: the sharp edge between two adjacent surfaces of a brick.

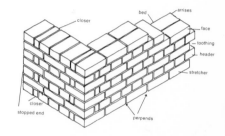

BAT: a broken section of a brick, larger than a quarter brick, used sometimes as an alternative to a closer (q.v.) in bonding and generally to make up dimensions in a wall.

BED JOINT: the horizontal joint between two courses of brickwork. A brick is bedded on mortar spread over the bricks below; the bottom horizontal surface of the brick is its bed (see diagram under ARRIS).

BLACK MORTAR: mortar containing crushed ashes in place of much of the sand normally used in the mix and giving a dark grey appearance; popular in the Industrial North and Midlands for its cheapness, its assumed weather resistance, and especially for the thin joints between machine-made pressed bricks.

BLIND WINDOW: a recess in a wall having jambs, head, sill, etc., formed in the brickwork but without a window-frame or glazing. Some such windows were blocked as a result of the window tax but many (probably most) were deliberately included as architectural details, especially by builders following copy-book designs.

39. *Blind window with cut brick flat arch, Heslington, Yorkshire, E.R.*

BLOCK BONDING: the use of several courses of brickwork at a time in joining one wall or part of a wall to another. Block bonding may also be used in the thickness of a wall, as where facing bricks are bonded to common bricks of different dimensions.

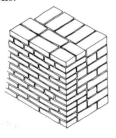

BLUE BRICKS: see STAFFORDSHIRE BLUE BRICKS.

BONDING: the regular arrangement of bricks in a pattern for strength or decoration.

AMERICAN BOND, etc.: see ENGLISH GARDEN-WALL BOND (below)

CHINESE BOND: see RAT-TRAP BOND (below)

DEARNE'S BOND (DEARNE'S HOLLOW WALL): the use of alternate courses of headers and bricks laid on edge in a 9-in thick wall. The headers act as ties, the bricks laid on edge have a 3-in cavity between. There is some saving of bricks over a solid wall and this bond was sometimes used for humble buildings and garden or boundary walls.

40. *Dearne's bond, Alton, Hampshire*

DUTCH BOND: a rare variation of Flemish bond (q.v., below) in which alternate courses are moved half a brick to left or right; also called staggered Flemish in the United States.

42. *English bond, Holy Trinity, Hull, Yorkshire, E.R.*

ENGLISH CROSS BOND: like English bond, but each alternate course of stretchers is moved over half a brick to give a stepped effect to the joints.

41. *Dutch bond, Capel, Surrey*

43. *English cross bond, Smallhythe, Kent*

ENGLISH BOND: a bond created from alternate courses of headers and stretchers. English bond is considered to be very strong because of the complete absence of straight joints within the wall, but it is more difficult to lay and more expensive than many other bonds.

ENGLISH GARDEN-WALL BOND: the use of either three or five courses of stretchers to one course of headers gives a bond which has many of the advantages of English bond but is much cheaper. It is one of the most popular of all brickwork bonds, especially in the North and Midlands. It is

sometimes called American bond, common bond, or Liverpool bond in the United States.

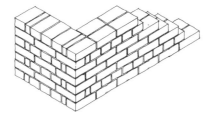

44. *English garden-wall bond, Heslington, Yorkshire, E.R.*

FLEMISH BOND : alternate headers and stretchers used in each course; considered to be more decorative but less strong than English bond and rarely seen in Flanders.

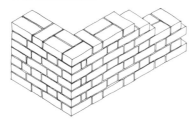

45. *Flemish bond with vitrified headers, Dorchester, Oxfordshire*

FLEMISH GARDEN-WALL BOND (SUSSEX BOND) : the use of three stretchers between each header in place of the single stretcher of Flemish bond.

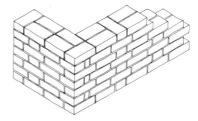

46. *Flemish garden-wall bond (Sussex bond), Barlwood, Surrey*

FLEMISH STRETCHER BOND : a bond in which courses of alternate headers and stretchers are separated by several courses of stretchers. Usually there are three courses of stretchers but there may be any number from one to six; sometimes called American with Flemish in the United States.

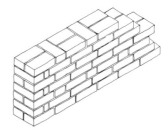

BONDING (*cont*)

47. *Flemish stretcher bond, Madeley, Shropshire*

HEADER BOND (HEADING BOND): the use of nothing but headers in each course of brickwork. Header bond was mainly employed for decorative effect, but has also been in demand for engineering work because of its great strength. This bond is useful for curved walls.

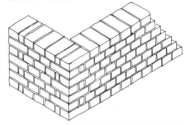

48. *Header bond on a curved wall, Beverley, Yorkshire, E.R.*

IRREGULAR BONDING: see p. 84

MIXED GARDEN BOND: a variation of Flemish stretcher bond in which headers do not lie above each other in any regular pattern.

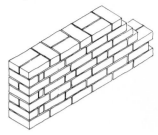

MONK BOND (FLYING BOND, YORKSHIRE BOND): a variation of Flemish bond with two stretchers instead of one between each header.

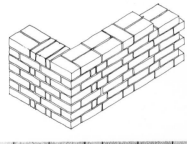

49. *Monk bond in concrete bricks, Oxford Road, Manchester*

RAKING STRETCHER BOND: as STRETCHER BOND (below), but with each brick overlapping the one below by a

71

quarter brick rather than the usual half brick.

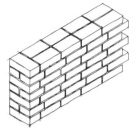

50. *Raking stretcher bond in metric bricks, Plymouth Grove, Manchester*

51. *Rat-trap bond, Colney Heath, Hertfordshire*

52. *Rat-trap Sussex bond, Farnham, Surrey*

RAT-TRAP BOND (CHINESE BOND, ROWLOCK BOND, SILVERLOCK BOND): a variation of Flemish bond, having alternate headers and stretchers in each course but with the bricks laid on edge instead of on bed. The resultant wall has a cavity between each pair of stretchers. Using fewer bricks to reach a given height, a wall built in rat-trap bond is cheaper than one in other bonds but is less strong and less weather resistant.

SINGLE FLEMISH BOND: gives the appearance of Flemish bond on the outside face only of a wall more than 9-in thick. Double Flemish bond gives the same appearance on both inner and outer faces.

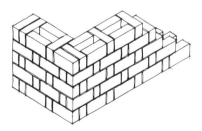

Double Flemish bond

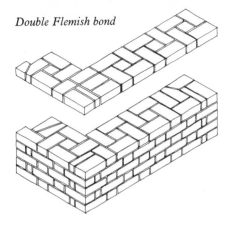

STACK BOND : courses of bricks on end with continuous vertical joints. Cannot be used in load-bearing walls.

53. *Stack bond, Grosvenor Street, Chester*

STRETCHER BOND : a bond consisting of bricks laid so that every course consists of stretchers only. It is the usual bond for cavity walls but is rarely used for solid walls because of the lack of bonding bricks running across the wall.

54. *Stretcher bond, Wilmslow, Cheshire : reused early 19th-century bricks*

SUSSEX BOND etc.: see FLEMISH GARDEN-WALL BOND (above)

YORKSHIRE BOND : see MONK BOND (above)

BOND TIMBERS : pieces of timber built into the inner face of a wall to provide horizontal reinforcement. They may be seen in agricultural or industrial buildings, but in houses they are generally concealed by plaster.

BREAKING JOINT : the avoidance of continuous vertical joints by laying the bricks in one course across the joints in the course below.

BRICK EARTH (BRICK CLAY) : strictly the term applies only to silty clays of the Pleistocene period found in parts of the Thames and Kennet valleys, Middlesex, East Anglia, the northern part of Kent, West Sussex, and the southern part of Hampshire, but in practice the term is generally applied to all clays from which bricks are made.

BRICK NOGGING : the use of bricks as in-filling between the members of a timber frame; it may be seen in external walls but may be concealed in internal partitions (see also *127*).

55. *Brick nogging, bricks laid on edge, Newtown, Montgomeryshire*

BRICK ON EDGE : the use of bricks laid on edge rather than on bed and displaying upright headers; commonly employed as a coping to a 9-in brick wall, as a sill, or for a flat arch.

56. *Brick on edge coping, Heslington, Yorkshire, E.R.*

BRICK ON END : the use of bricks on end rather than on bed and so displaying upright stretchers; commonly used for a flat arch, as a soldier course (q.v.) or generally for decorative purposes.

BRICK SLIPS : thin pieces of brick which have been specially moulded and fired to match the headers or stretchers of ordinary brickwork. They are used, for example, to cover concrete beams or stanchions in order to give the illusion of a continuous brick wall.

74

BRICK TAX: the tax levied on bricks in 1784 and repealed in 1850. At first the effects of the brick tax were reduced through the production of large-sized bricks (called tax bricks or great bricks), but later double tax was levied on bricks exceeding 150 cu in in volume, so that the only practical avoidance was through the use of mathematical tiles (brick-tiles q.v.) or other brick substitutes.

BRICK-TILES (MATHEMATICAL TILES, MECHANICAL TILES, WALL-TILES): tiles with one face moulded like the face or end of a brick. They were nailed to battens on a timber frame or other wall, or, occasionally, bedded into plaster rendering over cobble stones or pebbles, and were then pointed to look like bricks (see also 26).

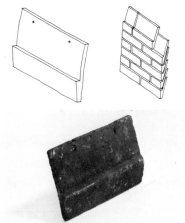

57. *Stretcher brick-tile (mathematical tile)*

58. *Header brick-tile (mathematical tile)*

59. *Glazed header brick-tile (mathematical tile)*

60. *Corner brick-tile (mathematical tile)*

61. *Brick-tile (mathematical tile) dated 1724, Westcott, Surrey*

BULLNOSE BRICKS: bricks with one arris (or occasionally two) rounded, and used where a sharp arris would be inconvenient or liable to damage.

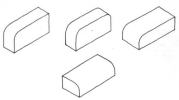

75

BULLSEYE : a small circular or oval window, opening, or blind panel; a popular device of the late 17th and early 18th centuries.

CAMBERED ARCH : an 'arch' whose upper edge (extrados) is horizontal but whose lower edge (intrados) is slightly curved in order to avoid the illusion of sagging.

62. Rubbed brick cambered arch, Knutsford, Cheshire

CARVED BRICKWORK : decoration created by carving solid brickwork rather than building up moulded bricks. Usually bricks similar to those for gauged brickwork were used but they were of larger dimensions, laid with fine joints, carved with hammer, bolster, etc., and then brought to the desired finish with a rubbing brick (see also *81*).

CAVITY WALL (HOLLOW WALL) : a wall built of two vertical leaves (q.v.) of bricks or blocks, separated by an air space, but linked by ties of galvanized wire or wrought iron. Traditionally the air space was kept quite free of any material lest a bridge for moisture penetration might be provided, but it is now quite common to fill the cavity with a material which improves insulation qualities while still acting as a moisture barrier.

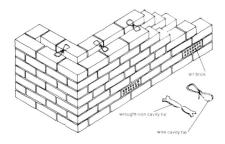

CEMENT MORTAR : mortar using Portland cement with sand as a partial or complete substitute for lime; it is stronger and more weather resistant than lime mortar but much inferior to it in appearance and suffers from shrinkage during setting. This mortar was often called 'compo' in the Victorian period, especially by the ecclesiologists, to indicate their contempt for it. This term is still current in the North.

CHEQUERED BRICKWORK : a regular pattern on the surface of a brick wall created, for example, through the use of flared or vitrified headers in Flemish bond. The term is also used of alternate squares or rectangles of brickwork and other material such as flint which may be mixed to give a kind of chessboard pattern.

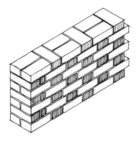

CHIMNEY : the structure containing a flue which served a fireplace. The chimney-*breast* contains the fireplace and may project into a room or out beyond an external wall; the chimney-*stack* takes one or more flues above roof level and may consist of a group of *shafts*, one to each flue (see also *114*).

63. *Plain and decorative chimney-stacks, The Manor House, Buckingham*

CHIMNEY-POT : a terracotta funnel terminating a flue and designed to improve the draught. There were very few in England before the reign of George III and the large majority are Victorian or later.

CHINESE BOND : see RAT-TRAP BOND, under BONDING

CLAMP : a stack of unburnt bricks made ready for firing.

CLOSER : a brick cut or moulded so as to expose a half-header and used to complete the bonding pattern at the return of a wall (see diagram under ARRIS). See also KING CLOSER and QUEEN CLOSER.

64. *Closer used with Flemish bond, Bluecoat School, Chester*

CLOSURE : a brick slip usually 2-in thick, acting with a header to provide the bond in early types of cavity wall.

COMMON BOND : see ENGLISH GARDEN-WALL BOND, under BONDING

COMMON BRICKS : ordinary cheap bricks not usually exposed nor used where great structural strength is needed. They often have surface imperfections such as 'kiss marks' (q.v.).

COMPO : see CEMENT MORTAR

CONCRETE BRICKS : bricks moulded from cement, sand, and some aggregate such as crushed stone. Unlike clay bricks they are not burnt in a kiln. They are used as common bricks in districts which lack clay or cheap fuel but are rough to handle and are easily chipped.

CORBELLING : projecting headers or courses (see also *136*).

65. *String course of corbelled headers and stretchers, Great Budworth, Cheshire*

CORBIE STEP : see CROW STEP

COSSEY WHITES : bricks, light yellow in colour, which were popular in and around Norwich about 1830.

COURSE : a horizontal layer of bricks.

CRINKLE-CRANKLE WALL : a garden wall which was usually only half a brick in thickness but which gained stability from serpentine curves on plan. Such walls are found mainly in East Anglia where they helped to provide some protection against the winds for the more delicate fruits, such as peaches or nectarines.

66. *Crinkle-crankle wall, Easton Park, Suffolk*

78

CROW STEP (CORBIE STEP): the finish of a gable parapet in a series of horizontal platforms like large steps. This detail was popular in 17th-century brickwork, especially in East Anglia. It was also used in other materials and other areas, for example in Scotland during the same period, where they were known as corbie steps.

67. *Crow-stepped gable, Barham Manor, Suffolk*

CUT BRICKS: bricks cut to shape with an axe or bolster, as distinct from those more precisely shaped by a rubber brick.

DAMP-PROOF COURSE: a horizontal layer of impervious material inserted in a brick wall to stop rising damp. Slate, asphalt, lead, and bituminous felt have commonly been used; also, less commonly, two courses of blue bricks (cf. STAFFORD-SHIRE BLUE BRICKS).

DEARNE'S BOND: see BONDING

DENTILATION: a tooth-like effect produced by the projection of alternate headers or smaller blocks. The detail is usually seen under a cornice, at eaves level, or at a string course (see also 75).

DIAPER: a pattern made by using bricks of two colours to form diamond, square, or lozenge shapes (see also 3).

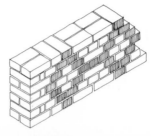

68. *Diapers at Christchurch Mansion, Ipswich, Suffolk*

DOG-LEG BRICKS: bricks specially made for use where two walls join at an obtuse angle, so as to avoid the use of cut bricks with straight joints and an uneven arris.

DOG-TOOTH BRICKWORK: a term sometimes given to the use of bricks laid diagonally to expose one corner as an alternative to the use of dentilation; also called HOUND'S-TOOTH or (in the United States) MOUSE-TOOTH.

69. *Dog-tooth brickwork and cut brick elliptical arch, Toft Green, York*

DRESSINGS: those parts of the walls of a building (such as door and window openings) carried out in a material superior to that used for the main walling. Dressings may be in a different substance, such as the Portland stone used with brickwork in many classically inspired buildings, or they may be in a superior version of the general walling material, as in the use of gauged brickwork with ordinary brickwork. Sometimes brick dressings are used with poor quality stone, flint, cobble, or pebble walls.

70. *Brick dressings to flint, Singleton, Sussex*

DUTCH BOND: see BONDING

DUTCH CLINKERS: small hard bricks, usually rather yellow in colour, brought as ballast in ships coming from the Netherlands during the second half of the 17th century and incorporated in brick walls near the ports of East Anglia or Kent, or used as paving bricks. This type of brick is also called klinkart.

DUTCH GABLE: a gable whose outline is composed of convex and concave curves, and sometimes crowned by a pediment (see *12, 68*).

EFFLORESCENCE: the powdery white deposit on the surface of new brickwork which comes from the drying out of salts in the bricks or mortar.

ENGINEERING BRICKS: dense bricks of uniform size and high crushing strength coupled with low porosity; as the name suggests, they have been employed mostly for structures such as railway viaducts, but because of their strength or uniformity they have also been used in buildings (see *31*).

ENGLISH BOND, ENGLISH CROSS BOND, ENGLISH GARDEN-WALL BOND: see BONDING

FACE: the exposed side of a brick (see diagram under ARRIS).

FACING BRICKS: bricks selected for use on the exposed surface of a wall because of their superior appearance to common bricks.

FLARED BRICKS: bricks laid as headers which are dark at one end through being placed close to the source of heat in a kiln and are used to form patterns in chequer or diaper work.

FLAT ARCH (STRAIGHT ARCH, FRENCH ARCH, JACK ARCH, SOLDIER ARCH): the use of a soldier course (q.v.) of bricks on edge or on end to make the head of an opening. The head is not arched in the true sense of the word, but the friction from the vertical joints gives something of the structural effect of an arch (see 39).

FLEMISH BOND, FLEMISH GARDEN-WALL BOND, FLEMISH STRETCHER BOND: see BONDING

FLEMISH BRICKS: thin bricks imported from the Low Countries or made locally in imitation of them.

FLETTONS: common bricks made from the Oxford Clays of the Peterborough district and widely used in the London area.

FLINT-LIME BRICKS: bricks made not of clay but of a mixture of lime and crushed flint baked in an oven. They are light in colour and usually weaker than clay bricks.

FLUSH JOINT: see JOINTING

FLUSH POINTING: see POINTING

FLYING BOND: see MONK BOND, under BONDING

FRENCH ARCH: see FLAT ARCH

FROG: an indentation in the surface of a brick which reduces its weight and so makes it easier to handle. Usually the brick is laid with the frog facing downwards. When it is laid 'frog up' the indentation must be filled with mortar by the bricklayer. Sometimes there are two frogs, one in each surface.

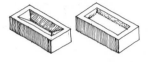

GALLETING: the use of pebbles or chips of stone pushed into mortar joints, probably for decoration but possibly for strengthening.

71. *Galleting, Shere, Surrey*

81

GAUGED BRICKWORK (RUBBED BRICKS):
the use of soft bricks sawn roughly to
shape and then rubbed to a smooth surface and precise (or gauged) dimensions
by a stone or another brick. Darker brick
colours and very fine joints of lime putty
(q.v.) are characteristic of gauged brickwork, which is most commonly found in
arches of doorways or window openings
(see also *16*).

72. *Gauged and moulded brickwork, Willmer
House, Farnham, Surrey*

GAULT BRICKS: bricks made from Gault
Clay (which is associated with chalk);
they are usually yellowish in colour but
may emerge as pink or red according to
their position in the kiln.

GLAZED BRICKS: bricks with shiny surfaces resulting from the application of a
salt glaze during firing; usually only one
end and one face are glazed. Such bricks
are used for situations where easy cleaning or light-reflecting qualities are important, or in the hope that a glazed brick
wall will be self-cleaning in the rain.

GREAT BRICKS: a term used in documents
to describe large thin bricks (e.g. $11 \times 12
\times 2$ in) used in medieval England.

73. *Mediaeval great brick, Waltham Abbey
Gatehouse, Essex*

GRIZZLES: grey bricks either made of
special clay and used as facings or underburnt bricks intended to be hidden or
used in an unobtrusive location.

HAND-MADE BRICKS: bricks moulded by
hand with the aid of a wooden mould
and stock-board before firing. Because
they are less uniform than machine-
made bricks they are sometimes preferred
for facings.

HEADER: a brick laid to expose one end
(or, in a 9-in garden wall, both ends) for
purposes of bonding or pattern making
(see diagram under ARRIS).

HEADER BOND, HEADING BOND: see
BONDING

HERRINGBONE BRICKWORK: bricks laid
not horizontally but diagonally and sloping in opposite directions. Herringbone
brickwork is used in brick nogging where
the timber frame is carrying the loads
(see diagram under BRICK NOGGING).

74. *Herringbone brick nogging,
Chiddingfold, Surrey*

HOFFMAN KILN: a type of kiln shaped
like an elongated circle and designed for
continuous production of bricks and
divided into several chambers. Each
chamber in turn is loaded with 'green'
bricks which are dried and burnt, cooled,
and removed, so that there is a batch of
new bricks produced every day. By
means of a system of ducts and flues the
heat from the continuously burning furnace is directed to firing and preheating,
while the waste heat from a chamber
which is cooling is used to help in drying
the 'green' bricks that have just been
loaded into another chamber.

HOLLOW WALL: an obsolete term for a
cavity wall.

HONEYCOMB BRICKWORK: the omission
of certain headers or stretchers in a brick
wall for purposes of ventilation or decoration; found in brick hay barns and in
the sleeper walls which carry the ground-
floor joists of most modern houses.

75. *Honeycomb brickwork, dentilated eaves,
Madeley, Shropshire*

83

76. *Honeycomb brickwork in barn at Adlington, Cheshire*

HOUND'S-TOOTH: see DOG-TOOTH BRICKWORK

IRREGULAR BONDING: brickwork given stability through the use of headers and broken vertical joints but without a regular bonding pattern (see also *98*).

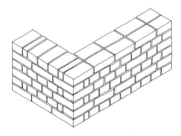

77. *Irregular bond, North Bar, Beverley, Yorkshire, E.R.*

78. *Irregular bond, Pershore, Worcestershire*

JACK ARCH: see FLAT ARCH

JOINTING: the use of mortar between adjacent bricks, horizontally and vertically as a spacing and bedding material.

FLUSH JOINT: a mortar joint which has been made flush with the surface of the brickwork.

KEYED JOINT: a term used to describe both a joint left recessed or raked out to receive plaster or stucco and a joint pointed and finished to a concave section.

RAKED-OUT JOINT: a joint which has been cleared of mortar to a depth of $\frac{1}{2}$ in or $\frac{3}{4}$ in from the face of the brickwork. This may be done for decorative reasons or to form a key for subsequent rendering.

RUBBED JOINT: a flush joint which the bricklayer has made by rubbing excess mortar off the surface of the brickwork with a piece of rag, rubber or some comparable material.

SCORED JOINT (RULED JOINT): a joint in which grooves have been impressed by running the point of the trowel against a straight-edge (i.e. a piece of wood about 3 ft long with smooth, straight, parallel edges) so as to give the appearance of very fine precise brickwork.

79. *Flemish bond, scored joint, off Micklegate, York*

STRUCK JOINT: a joint with mortar pressed in at the bottom (like a weathered joint upside down), characteristic of bricks laid overhand from within a building rather than in the normal way from outside.

WEATHERED JOINT: a joint in which the mortar (or the pointing mortar if used) has been pressed in at the top by the bricklayer's trowel.

KING CLOSER: a three-quarter bat with half a header exposed as a closer. The brick is often given a diagonal cut back from the exposed half-header, but this is hidden within the thickness of the wall.

KISS MARKS: discolorations of the surface of bricks resulting from the method of stacking unfired bricks on top of each other in the clamp or kiln.

KLINKART: see DUTCH CLINKERS

LACING COURSE: One or more courses of bricks serving as horizontal reinforcement to walls of flint, cobble, pebble, or some other awkwardly shaped material.

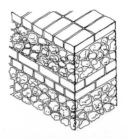

80. *Pebble wall with brick lacing course, Lewes, Sussex*

LAP: in bonding, the projection of one brick over the one below.

LEAF: the thin brick wall which forms an element of a cavity wall; there are an inner leaf and an outer leaf of brickwork as well as the cavity between.

LIME MORTAR: a mixture usually consisting of about one part slaked lime to six parts sand, though sometimes with the addition of a little cement.

LIME PUTTY: lime mortar without sand or cement: quicklime slaked and sieved (*82*).

LIVERPOOL BOND: see ENGLISH GARDEN-WALL BOND, under BONDING

85

LOUDON'S HOLLOW WALL: an 11-in wall in Flemish bond with a 2-in cavity between stretchers and a 2-in closure (q.v.) behind each header.

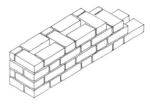

MATHEMATICAL TILES, MECHANICAL TILES: see BRICK-TILES

METRIC BRICKS: bricks made to metric dimensions, e.g. 215 × 107·5 × 65 mm.

MIXED GARDEN BOND: see BONDING

MODILLIONS: small projecting brackets, usually in series below a cornice.

81. *Carved and rubbed brick modillions, Chiddingfold, Surrey*

MONK BOND: see BONDING

MORTAR: the material used in bedding one brick upon another and in jointing and pointing generally (cf. BLACK MORTAR, CEMENT MORTAR, LIME MORTAR).

MOULDED BRICKWORK: the use of bricks moulded to a selected shape before firing and built up to make ornamental architectural details (see also *72, 105*).

82. *Detail of moulded brickwork and polychromy, Bradbourne, Larkfield, Kent*

MOUSE-TOOTH: see DOG-TOOTH BRICKWORK

NOGGING: see BRICK NOGGING

PAMMENTS: thin paving bricks between about 9 in and 12 in square.

PATTERNED BRICKWORK: see CHEQUERED BRICKWORK and DIAPER

PAVING BRICKS (PAVIOUR BRICKS):
bricks of special composition and dimensions to serve as paving; designed for hard wear, low porosity, and resistance to frost.

83. *Paving bricks, Ironbridge, Shropshire*

PERFORATED BRICKS: vertical perforations introduced into bricks to save weight without significantly reducing strength.

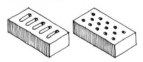

PERPENDS: the vertical joints visible in a brick wall. It is good bricklaying practice to keep perpends directly above each other in each alternate course (see diagram under ARRIS).

PLACE BRICKS: cheap underburnt red bricks used as commons rather than as facings.

PLAT BAND: a rectangular moulding of shallow projection usually denoting externally the horizontal division between the storeys. On a brick building it may be of brick, stone, or stucco (see *111, 133*) cf. STRING COURSE.

PLINTH BRICK: a brick chamfered on face or end to provide for the reduction in thickness between the plinth and the main part of a wall.

POINTING: the application of a superior mortar to the raked-out joints of ordinary mortar.

FLUSH POINTING: pointing the joints of a brick wall but scraping the mortar smooth with a trowel, a rag, a piece of rubber, etc., in order to obtain a uniform wall surface.

TUCK POINTING: a method of pointing in which a lime putty, usually white but sometimes black, is inserted into a pointing mortar which matches or is darker than the brick colour, giving the illusion, until it begins to fall out (as in the course of time it usually does), of very fine, precise joints.

84. *Flemish bond, with tuck pointing, Tanner Row, York*

POLYCHROME BRICKWORK: the use of several colours for decorative effect. The term is usually applied to 19th-century work with, for example, arch-voussoirs of different colours following Italian Gothic precedents (see *33, 82*).

PRESSED BRICKS: bricks moulded under high pressure before firing, to give smooth surfaces and sharp arrises.

PROJECTING HEADERS: patterning like diaper work (q.v.), but made by using projecting headers of ordinary brickwork.

85. Decorative shape in projecting headers, Great Budworth, Cheshire

PURPOSE-MADE BRICKS: bricks which have been moulded to a special shape, usually to deal with a specific building problem. Where, for instance, a wall was to be built to an irregular plan, purpose-made bricks would be required to give a neat finish at the corners.

PUTLOG HOLES (PUTLOCK HOLES): the recesses left in a brick wall to receive the horizontal bearers of scaffolding. These holes should normally be filled in as the scaffolding is taken down, but sometimes this was not done, or the loose brickbats used as infill dropped out, revealing the putlog holes.

QUEEN CLOSER: a half-bat or two quarter-bats cut to show a half-header width.

QUOINS: groups of bricks projecting from the general surface of the building at its corners in imitation of the corner stones of a masonry building (see *116*).

RACKING (RACKING BACK): reducing the height of a brick wall in steps from a corner or termination. The corners of brick walls are usually raised first to ensure perfectly vertical lines and horizontal courses; the walls are racked back from the corners for subsequent completion (see diagram under STRETCHER BOND, p. 73).

RAKED-OUT JOINT: see JOINTING

RAKING STRETCHER BOND: see BONDING

RAT-TRAP BOND : see BONDING

RECESSED JOINT : see JOINTING

RELIEVING ARCH : an arch built within a wall above an opening and transmitting loads to the sides of the opening in order to relieve the lintel or flat arch at its head.

86. *Segmental relieving arch, rubbed brick architrave, flat arch, Balls Park, Hertfordshire*

RENDERED BRICKWORK : brickwork covered externally by some variation of plaster. The finish may be stucco, i.e. lime/sand or lime/cement/sand brought to a very smooth finish; or it may be roughcast, i.e. coarse sand or washed gravel mixed with slaked lime and thrown on; or it may be pebble-dash, i.e. small washed pebbles thrown on to wet cement. There are other finishes which have been used occasionally.

ROMAN BRICKS : the thin tile-like bricks used by the Romans and reused for later buildings on Roman sites, as at Colchester (see *97*).

ROUGH BRICK ARCH : an arch made up of bricks which have not been moulded or cut to voussoir shape. The necessary taper is provided in the mortar joints. Such arches are usually made of one or two rings of brick on edge.

87. *Rough brick surround to cast-iron plaque, Madeley, Shropshire*

ROWLOCK : an American term for laying bricks on edge rather than on bed; thus rowlock bond is the same as rat-trap bond.

RUBBED BRICK : see GAUGED BRICKWORK

RUBBED JOINT : see JOINTING

RULED JOINT : see SCORED JOINT, under JOINTING

RUSTIC BRICK : a facing brick with surfaces (often only one end and one face) which have been improved by a sand covering or a scratched pattern before firing. They are often given variegated colours at the same time.

RUSTICATION: in stonework, a method of emphasizing each block by surrounding it with deeply recessed joints to yield shadows. Sometimes imitated in brickwork by sinking every fourth or fifth mortar course and by chamfering the edges of the adjacent bricks.

SADDLE-BACK COPING BRICK: a purpose-made brick with top bed sloping in two directions.

SAMMEL BRICKS: rough-textured under-fired bricks, pinkish in colour.

SAND-FACED BRICKS: bricks with one face and one end sanded before firing, to give a rough-textured finish.

SAND-LIME BRICKS: bricks made not of clay but of sand with slaked lime, and then baked to a light grey or near-white colour.

SCORED JOINT: see JOINTING

SEGMENTAL ARCH: an arch in which the underside (intrados) and the upper edge (extrados) of the bricks form segments struck from the same centre. It may be a rough arch or one formed out of moulded or gauged-brick voussoirs.

88. *Rough brick segmental arch, Chiddingfold, Surrey*

SHALE: hard laminated rocks which may be crushed or broken down through weathering and mixed with mortar so as to form a plastic mass from which bricks may be moulded and fired. Suitable shales are found in the coalfields, especially of Durham, Yorkshire, Lancashire and Staffordshire.

SILVERLOCK BOND: see RAT-TRAP BOND, under BONDING

SINGLE FLEMISH BOND: see BONDING

SKEWBACK: the backward sloping voussoir at the springing of a flat arch.

SNAP HEADERS: half-bats with one end exposed and used to provide a bonding pattern in the outer leaf of a cavity wall.

SOLDIER ARCH: see FLAT ARCH

SOLDIER COURSE: a course of bricks laid on end, standing upright like soldiers (see also *111*).

SPECIALS: purpose-made bricks of non-standard shape, e.g. Bullnose bricks (q.v.).

SPRINGER: the first brick on each side of an arch. In a flat arch it may incline backwards as a skewback.

STACK BOND: see BONDING

90

STAFFORDSHIRE BLUE BRICKS: hard dense bricks varying in colour from slate-grey through all the darker blues to deep purple, made out of Staffordshire shales. They were intended for engineering or industrial purposes, and much employed for damp-proof courses. Used, especially in the 1960s, for other buildings too. See also ENGINEERING BRICKS.

STOCK BRICK: a term applied to any brick hand-made with the aid of a brick stock, a wooden board on which a frame was placed to contain the clay. It is also used to describe the ordinary brick of a locality, nowadays most frequently with reference to the yellowish-brown bricks of the London area (see *22, 133*).

STOPPED END: a wall brought to a neat termination with the aid of closers (see diagram under ARRIS).

STRAIGHT ARCH: see FLAT ARCH

STRAIGHT JOINTS: vertical joints which are directly above other vertical joints, i.e. without another brick in between, a situation avoided in proper bonding.

STRETCHER: a brick placed on bed to expose one long face (see diagram under ARRIS).

STRETCHER BOND: see BONDING

STRING COURSE: a horizontal projecting band, sometimes of dentilated or dog-tooth brickwork, and usually at an intermediate floor level (see *17, 115*) cf. PLAT BAND.

STRUCK JOINT: see JOINTING

SUSSEX BOND: see FLEMISH GARDEN-WALL BOND, under BONDING

TAX BRICKS: bricks of larger than normal dimensions made to evade the early brick tax, which was levied simply on the number of bricks made. Subsequent legislation eliminated the advantage of using very large bricks (which were in any case difficult and expensive to lay), but bricks thicker than had been normal remained in use, especially in the North and Midlands. See also GREAT BRICKS.

TERRACOTTA: burnt clay of uniform and fine-textured material. It can be glazed or unglazed, and may be moulded to provide architectural details. The blocks of terracotta are usually hollow (see also *103*).

89. *Terracotta ornamentation to doorway on south front, Sutton Place, Surrey*

90. *Terracotta dressings to window, Sutton Place, Surrey*

91. *Tie plate, Beverley, Yorkshire, E.R.*

TILE: a square or rectangular piece of burnt clay thinner than a brick.

TILE CREASING: the use of one or two courses in a wall, e.g. under a coping or under a sill, for decorative or damp-proofing purposes (see *36*).

92. *Tie plate, Ironbridge, Shropshire*

TIE RODS and TIE PLATES: wrought-iron rods threaded through buildings and with plates of various shapes at each end. They were tightened to prevent brick walls from bellying out. More elaborate ties were used where there were poor foundations, e.g. through subsidence.

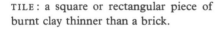

93. *Tie plate, Shere, Surrey*

94. *Tie plate, Westcott, Surrey.*

TOOTHING : bricks projecting like teeth in alternate courses in order to bond with other brickwork (see diagram under ARRIS) cf. BLOCK BONDING.

TUCK POINTING : see POINTING

TUMBLING-IN : the term used to describe courses of brickwork laid at right angles to the slope of a gable or chimney-breast and tapering into horizontal courses (see also *112*).

95. *Gable with 'tumbling-in', Cherry Burton, Yorkshire, E.R.*

VITRIFIED HEADERS : bricks which have been given a dark glaze at one end by being placed in the hottest part of the kiln or through the addition of salt during the burning process.

VOUSSOIRS : wedge-shaped bricks used in the construction of arches, including flat or cambered arches.

96. *Voussoirs in flat and segmental gauged-brick arches, Farnham, Surrey*

WALL-TILES : see BRICK-TILES

WEATHERED JOINT : see JOINTING

WEEP-HOLE : a vertical joint left without mortar to drain water away from a cavity wall above a damp-proof course.

WIRE-CUT BRICK : brick clay extruded through an aperture and cut (like cheese) into brick shapes by wires and then burnt in the kiln. Wire-cut bricks are less dense than pressed bricks; they may be perforated but do not have a frog, and often show on the surface the parallel lines resulting from the extrusion process.

YORKSHIRE BOND : see MONK BOND, under BONDING

Three

Chronological Survey

This section illustrates the use of brickwork, period by period, from the Middle Ages to the present day. The examples have been chosen to illustrate the use of brickwork in buildings as a whole as well as to show the development of details in brickwork.

A wide range of building types has been illustrated, with emphasis on those which are characteristic of their particular period: parish churches show late mediaeval brickwork, country houses demonstrate the remarkable skills of the Georgian craftsmen, and the nineteenth and twentieth centuries are represented largely by public, commercial and industrial buildings. At the same time the examples have been chosen from the regions and counties particularly notable for them – the Eastern Counties, Kent and others for early brickwork, London and the great industrial cities for the later work in brick.

By following the sequence of illustrations the reader should obtain an overall picture of the changing use of brick from its early beginnings as a fairly crude alternative to stone through its development as a building material in its own right to its subsequent further evolution as a decorative material with which bricklayers, architects and sculptors have exercised skills of the highest order.

OPPOSITE 97. *St Botolph's Priory, Colchester, Essex. Late 11th century; thin Roman bricks; wide joints; structural arches and interlaced arcading.*

RIGHT 98. *North Bar, Beverley, Yorkshire, E.R. Rebuilt 1409; thin bricks (2 in) varying in length; irregular bonding; 'squynchons' or chamfered bricks in jambs and arches; moulded bricks for cusped ogee arches over the niches.*

99. *The Deanery, Hadleigh, Suffolk. 1495; English bond; some diaper work; terracotta cusped heads to arches over panels; central windows and chimney-stack later.*

100. *The Deanery, Hadleigh, Suffolk : north-east turret. Quality of bonding lost at back of walls; bricks used as weathering on battlements are held in place by bricks on edge; repointing mars upper part.*

ABOVE 101. *Hampton Court Palace, Middlesex : Anne Boleyn's Gateway. 1520 and later; English bond modified for diaper work; terracotta medallions; repairs in Flemish bond.*

OPPOSITE 102. *St Mary, Stoke-by-Nayland, Suffolk : north porch. Probably early 16th century; irregular-sized bricks laid in approximately English cross bond; cut brick mullions and tracery probably plastered originally.*

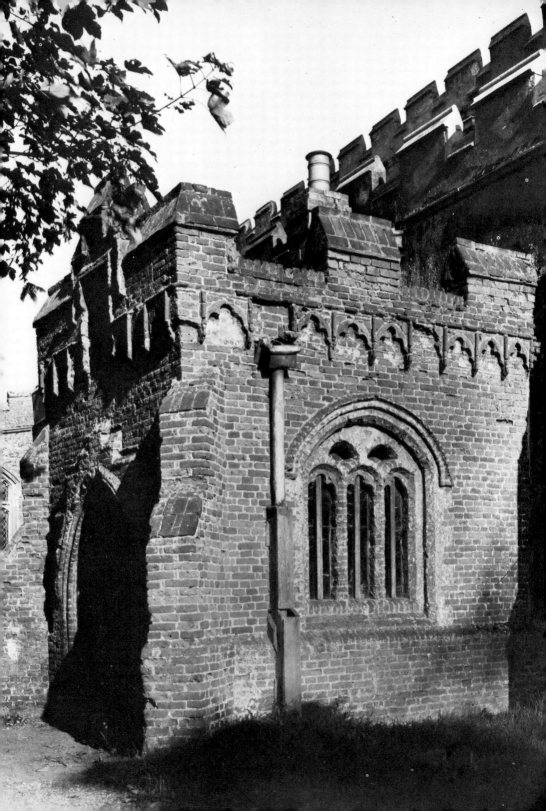

103. *Sutton Place, Surrey : south front. c. 1530 ; English bond modified for diaper work ; terracotta dressings and panels.*

ABOVE 104. *St Michael, Woodham Walter,*
Essex : west wall. 1564; lower part has an
irregular bond consisting mainly of
stretchers with occasional headers; upper
part is in Flemish stretcher bond, unusual
in its early date and also in the use of only
one course of stretchers between courses of
alternate headers and stretchers.

RIGHT 105. *Roos Hall, Beccles, Suffolk :*
doorway. 1593; four-centred arches; hood
mould and label stops in cut and moulded
brick; English bond.

106. *Burton Constable, Yorkshire, E.R. : part of east front. Late 16th century;*
English bond; stone dressing; I-shaped tie plates.

TOP 107. *Bramshill House, Hampshire: south-west front. 1605–12; English bond; stone dressings; blind windows at basement level.*

BOTTOM 108. *Quenby Hall, Leicestershire: west front. c. 1615–36; stone plinth and dressings; diaper pattern; generally English bond; top storey of porch later and with header pattern in Flemish bond.*

OPPOSITE 109. *Wilberforce House, Hull, Yorkshire, E.R.: doorway and niches. c. 1630; brickwork extravagantly though rather crudely cut and shaped so that the whole front is modelled; bricks thin (2 in) but with wide joints (four courses rise $10\frac{1}{2}$ in) laid generally in English bond.*

RIGHT 110. *Halghton Hall, Flintshire. Stone plinth and dressings; bricks of irregular length; English bond but very inconsistent.*

BELOW 111. *Brunger, Leigh Green, Tenterden, Kent. Late 16th–early 17th century; tall central chimney-stack with simple oversailing courses at the cap; soldier courses for window-heads and sills; plat band of two courses; English bond.*

TOP 112. *Cottage adjoining Badley Hall, Badley, Suffolk: chimney-breast. During the late 16th century and throughout the 17th century brickwork was used in small houses and cottages for internal or external chimney-breasts and stacks in association with timber-frame construction. Here the 'tumbling-in' of the offsets is noteworthy.*

BOTTOM 113. *The Old School, Boxford, Suffolk: chimney-stack. Probably late 16th century; bricks set diagonally on a battlemented base.*

OPPOSITE 114. *House at Charlwood, Surrey: chimney-breast. Base English bond; main part Flemish bond; stack stretcher bond.*

BELOW 115. *Balls Park, Hertfordshire : garden front. c. 1640; cut and rubbed brick dressings; segmental relieving arches over ground-floor windows; English bond generally.*

OPPOSITE 116. *Balls Park, Hertfordshire : corner of garden front. Fairly thin bricks (2¼ in) with thick joints (four courses rise 10¾ in) ; intermediate cornice made of rubbed, moulded, and ordinary bricks; chamfered bricks simulate rusticated quoins.*

OPPOSITE TOP 117. *Tyttenhanger Park, Hertfordshire. c. 1660; pediments, architraves, quoins, string courses, all in carved or rubbed brickwork; Flemish bond generally.*

OPPOSITE BOTTOM 118. *Hampton Court Palace, Middlesex : south front. Part of the Wren work of c. 1689–1702; all the dressings are in Portland stone standing out from the red brick of the main wall; Flemish bond.*

ABOVE 119. *Tredegar House, Monmouthshire : side view. Later 17th century; stone dressings to carefully laid English bond brickwork.*

ABOVE 120. *Old Meeting House, Norwich, Norfolk. 1693; only the capitals and bases are in stone; the rest, including the taper and entasis of the pilasters, is executed in brick; Flemish bond.*

OPPOSITE 121. *Bailey Hall, Hertford : detail of window. Early 18th century; white brick in Flemish bond; red brick around windows; bricks fairly thick ($2\frac{1}{2}$ in); cambered arch in gauged brick; red gauged brick pilasters in English bond.*

OPPOSITE 122. *Houghton Hall, Norfolk : vault of stables. c. 1730; the groined vaulting is most ingeniously contrived in brickwork; the proportion of headers increases as the crown of the vault is approached; bricks are cut and almost dovetailed together to form the groin or intersection of the vaults.*

ABOVE 123. *Holkham Hall, Norfolk : south front. 1734–61, by William Kent; yellow brick; Flemish bond; plain, almost unadorned surfaces.*

RIGHT 124. *Holkham Hall, Norfolk : detail of rustication. Effect of masonry from bricks moulded to provide the chamfering in the rustication.*

125. *Matfield House, Kent. 1728; semicircular and segmental arches in rubbed brick of bright red against deep plum colour of the main wall; Flemish bond.*

126. *Sherman House, Dedham, Essex. c. 1735; main wall Flemish bond; architectural details in rubbed and gauged brick so fine that the joints are almost invisible; the red gauged brickwork stands out from the white brick body of the main wall; note dentilation under cornice.*

127. *Hafod-y-Bwlch, Denbighshire. A modest timber-framed house, much enlarged, probably mid-18th century, by the addition of a wing in thick irregular bricks; massive chimney-stacks with decorative sunk panels; whitewashed brick nogging replaces original wattle and daub.*

128. *Rectory, Church Langton, Leicestershire. Built shortly before 1800;
semicircular and flat arches of gauged brick over windows; main walling Flemish
bond.*

129. *90 West Street, Farnham, Surrey. Mid-18th century; very plain brickwork; Flemish bond with English bond at the base; flat arches to windows.*

130. *1 Duke Street, Hadleigh, Suffolk. Late 18th century; Flemish bond; bricks rather thick; shallow gauged brick flat arches to ground-floor windows.*

ABOVE 131. *Sir John Leman's School, Beccles, Suffolk. 1631 and 1762, with early 19th-century alterations; principal wall of flint diapered with brick headers; English bond brickwork in gable wall.*

OPPOSITE 132. *House in Southernhay, Exeter, Devon. 1798; one of a terrace; some Coade stone dressings around the door; Flemish bond; semicircular arches of gauged brick over ground-floor windows.*

124

OPPOSITE 133. *9–10 Selwood Place, South Kensington, London. Early 19th century; stucco for ground floor and for window reveals; cambered cut brick arches to window-heads; yellow-brown London stock brick; Flemish bond generally, but later extension for mansard roof is in English bond.*

ABOVE 134. *Burton Constable, Yorkshire, E.R.: stables. c. 1760; simple but carefully modelled elevation depending on plain brickwork; stretcher bond generally, with occasional header courses; gauged brick for semicircular arches.*

135. *Village Farm, Seighford, Staffordshire : dovecot. 1758 ; corbelled headers and stretchers in brickwork generally of Sussex bond; below, headers omitted to provide ventilation.*

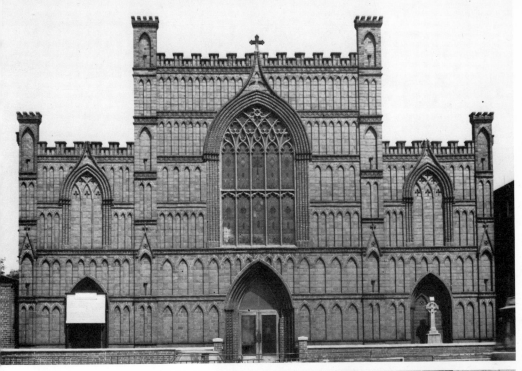

136. *Holy Trinity Church,
Newcastle-under-Lyme,
Staffordshire. 1833, by Egan;
unusual use of deep purple near-
glazed bricks in a boldly panelled
west front.*

137. *Holy Trinity Church,
Newcastle-under-Lyme : detail.
Wide, thin paving-type bricks laid
on edge, with lacing courses in a
somewhat darker tone.*

OPPOSITE 138. *The Red House, Bexleyheath, Kent. 1859, designed by Philip Webb for William Morris; generally English bond with header bond for the well head; two ring cut brick arches to the bullseye windows, pointed relieving arches over segmental arched heads.*

BELOW 139. *Keble College, Oxford. 1868–82, by Butterfield; polychrome brickwork in red, yellow, and slate-blue and with sandstone dressings.*

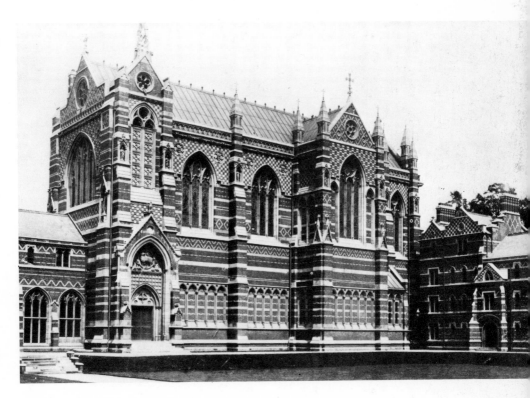

OPPOSITE 140. *Royal Holloway College, near Egham, Surrey. Built 1879–87 to designs by W. H. Crossland developing the Château of Chambord into hard red brick; English bond; plain walls relieved by cylindrical turrets and white stone dressings.*

ABOVE 141. *Refuge Assurance Company Building, Oxford Street, Manchester. 1891–1912, by P. Waterhouse; very hard thin bricks with precise blackened mortar joints; generally English bond; elaborate terracotta dressings; top of tower in yellowish terracotta.*

OPPOSITE 142. *Clock House, Chelsea Embankment, London. Built 1879 by Norman Shaw; walls of Flemish bond with dressings of moulded brick in deeper colour.*

RIGHT 143. *Westminster Cathedral, Ashley Place, Victoria, London. 1895–1903, by J. F. Bentley; red brick and some tile; stone dressings; the tower is illustrated here, but the walls generally are in a variation of English garden-wall bond in which the second and fourth stretcher courses are offset by a quarter brick length instead of a half brick.*

OPPOSITE 144. *Gladstone Pottery, Longton, Staffordshire: bottle kilns. Mid-19th century; some of the few remaining examples of once common brick structures; heat inside and rain outside mean that kilns are easily cracked and so have to be bound with iron hoops and frequently repointed; English garden-wall bond, but the tapered shape makes it difficult to avoid straight joints.*

TOP 145. *Alder Mill, Leigh, Lancashire: cotton spinning mill. Built 1907; red brick for the piers and spandrels; yellow brick for cambered arches and sills; Art Nouveau decoration in yellow terracotta seen especially in the water tower on the right.*

BOTTOM 146. *Shakespeare Memorial Theatre, Stratford-upon-Avon, Warwickshire. 1928–32, by Elizabeth Scott; plain brickwork in boldly massed blocks relieved by soldier courses, pilasters, and other projections in brick; the original appearance is shown in this illustration.*

OPPOSITE 147. *Odeon Cinema, York. 1936, by H. Weedon; Dutch influence; flat planes but with recessed courses, curved bands, and columns of brick set diagonally; buff bricks; thin (2 in) and mainly in Sussex bond.*

BELOW 148. *The Mond Laboratory, Cambridge. 1933; Eric Gill's representation of a crocodile has been cut on a wall whose regular network of joint lines for Flemish bond offsets the flow of incised lines for the sculptural relief.*

ABOVE 149. *The Cathedral, Guildford, Surrey. 1936–61, by Sir Edward Maufe; tall massive walls of brickwork in monk bond and with few stone dressings.*

OPPOSITE 150. *Office Building, Bow Street, Manchester. 1971; concrete bricks used in a boldly modelled pattern to form a non-structural screen wall, part solid, part honeycombed.*

151. *New Fountain Brewery, Edinburgh. 1973, designed by the Architects Department, Scottish and Newcastle Breweries Ltd; showing use of non-structural brickwork in which industrial requirements have led to the use of unusual forms, achieved in brickwork with the aid of many 'specials'.*

142

Appendix A

The Cavity Wall in Brickwork

The cavity wall is surely, for the majority, the most familiar of all types of brick wall. Its endlessly repetitive stretcher bond extends for miles between the picture windows and weather-boarded panels of suburbia from Carlisle to Cowes. But the cavity wall deserves special mention in any study of brickwork because, in spite of its recent widespread use, it only came into general favour in the 1920s and seems likely to pass out of use in its most familiar form in the 1970s. It is, therefore, a type of construction which has developed, flourished, and been abandoned in the lifetime of many readers.

The brick cavity wall consists of three elements: an inner and an outer leaf of brickwork and an air space in between. The outer leaf of facing bricks deflects the rain and carries some of the loads; the inner leaf of common bricks provides a key for the plaster lining, gives stability to the outer leaf, and carries the rest of the load; the air space prevents moisture which may pass through the outer leaf from being absorbed into the inner leaf, allows for the evaporation of moisture from either of the brickwork leaves, and provides some heat insulation. The two leaves are tied together and the cavity bridged by metal ties, usually of galvanized steel wire, but otherwise the three elements are kept separate and the cavity maintained unbroken and continuous throughout the wall.

There seem to have been four possible origins for the cavity wall:

1. the various bonds, principally rat-trap bond, which use bricks laid on edge to produce a discontinuous cavity in a wall 9-in or 11-in thick;

2. the use of a separate layer either outside the main structural wall to deflect driving rain or inside the main wall to conceal dampness;

3. the impression that a cavity would act as a heat insulator and might be used to distribute hot air;

4. the experiments with hollow blocks of various sorts which, combining damp resistance and light weight, could be as easily handled as conventional bricks but with greater economy.

Of these four possible origins, the first was abandoned because of the poor damp resistance of walls in which bricks acted as cavity ties, the fourth has continued intermittently as a series of experiments the results of which have never found real favour, while the second and third have combined to produce the cavity wall with which we are familiar.

There is no mention of hollow-wall or cavity-wall construction in the seventeenth-century technical works such as Moxon's *Mechanick Exercises* nor in the eighteenth-century architectural pattern books such as that of Batty Langley; and it was not until the early nineteenth century that the idea was introduced. In his *Views of Picturesque Cottages with Plans* published in 1805, William Atkinson recommended that 'in constructing walls for cottages or other edifices in brick a great saving might be made in materials without sacrificing much in regard to strength by leaving the walls hollow'. Two leaves with a 6-in cavity and brick ties were suggested, and it was pointed out that 'a hollow wall will be much warmer also than any other kind in consequence of the air confined in the cavity which is one of the best non-conductors of heat and cold'.[1] Thus stability, economy and insulating properties were linked as advocates for the cavity wall at this early date, and its connection with very small dwellings – cottage property – was established. In the present early stages of research into brickwork it is impossible to tell how far, if at all, Atkinson's recommendations were followed by his readers. Thomas Dearne, however, recommended a somewhat similar form of construction shortly afterwards in his *Hints on an Improved Method in Building* published in 1821, but with the modern 11-in width of two $4\frac{1}{2}$-in brick leaves and a 2-in cavity, the two leaves being tied by headers with 2-in closures in the inner leaf.[2] Again one cannot be sure how popular this technique proved to be, except that the author has given his name to Dearne's bond, one version of which is as described in the Glossary. In 1839 an ingenious variation of the hollow-wall idea was suggested by S. H. Brooks in his *Designs for Cottage and Villa Architecture* (the book is undated, but the plates are dated 1839).[3] In a design for a cottage 'in the Italian Style' it is proposed 'to erect the walls hollow by carrying up $4\frac{1}{2}$-in brickwork externally and internally, leaving a cavity between them of 5 in. The bond of the brickwork is to be made by bricks 14 in by 9 in, which may be placed at every fifth or seventh stretcher horizontally and in every third or fifth course vertically. In this way an excellent bond may be obtained, and if the sides of the openings be pargetted in the same manner as fireplace flues they may be made to carry rarefied air to all the apartments; and with suitable ventilators the rooms may be kept at an equable temperature, which cannot be done with a common English fireplace.' The cool air was to be admitted by way of grilles near the base of the wall and heated by means of a hot iron plate behind the fireplace. The idea is reminiscent of the Gravity Warm Air Heating System officially recommended after 1945, and would probably have been no more successful. However, the idea of using a wide cavity as a warm-air duct was applied to the 'peach wall' in some late nineteenth-century gardens in which air from a furnace at one end was drawn along a garden wall to heat the surfaces against which the fruit trees were trained.

In the second half of the nineteenth century more advocates of the cavity wall emerged. In H. Roberts's report on *The Dwellings of the Labouring Classes* (1850), as well as various hollow bricks, the use of 11-in cavity walls with brick ties and 2-in 'closures' as in Dearne's bond was recommended.[4] The cavity-wall idea was understood in America at this time; its introduction was credited to Ithiel Town, who trained under Asher Benjamin and who used the construction widely in New Haven, Connecticut.[5] There it attracted the attention of A. J. Downing, who was an enthusiastic advocate of a technique which he believed would save materials, avoid dampness, conserve heat, and eliminate the need for furring and lathing for interior plasterwork. His contemporary, Gilbert Vaux, continued the advocacy in *Villas and Cottages*, 1867, but was more cautious: 'a wall eight inches thick with a hollow space of 3, 4, or 5 inches and an inner wall of 4 inches is the thinnest hollow wall that can properly be built'.[6] He understood the value of a slate damp-proof course and iron ties and insisted that 'the two thicknesses of brick must be entirely and totally distinct if a satisfactory result is to be aimed at'. It is curious that he made the outer leaf load-bearing and the inner leaf simply damp-excluding, whereas we tend to transpose the two roles. In Britain the same techniques were advocated by J. J. Stevenson in *House Architecture*, Vol. II, published in 1880; he had, in fact already put this idea into practice at 8 Palace Gate, S.W.7., which was one of the earliest examples of cavity-wall construction in London. The 'hollow space' gave dry walls, provided the two leaves were not tied together by 'absorbent bricks or stones which would concentrate the moisture on the inner wall on the spots where they occur', and kept the house cool in summer and warm in winter especially if the inner leaf were only half a brick thick and the outer as thick as possible beyond the air space.[7]

The Papworth edition of *Gwilt's Encyclopaedia of Architecture* summarized and illustrated cavity-wall construction as understood in the 1860s:

a. rat-trap bond employed for some two-storey cottages since early in the century;
b. English bond with stretchers cut in half longitudinally so as to give a $4\frac{1}{2}$-in cavity in each alternate course (a most unsatisfactory and improbable form of construction);
c. cavity-wall construction as we now know it with wrought-iron cramps, a technique used, apparently, in Southampton.[8]

The debate about ventilated as opposed to unventilated cavities had already begun. Also illustrated was the 'air drain', a cavity wall around basements, the outer leaf being $4\frac{1}{2}$ in and the inner the thickness required for the stability of the wall. While 'hollow walls' were specified for exposed situations a 'hollow wall' was defined as one 'built in two thicknesses leaving a cavity between them for the purpose of saving materials or for preserving a uniform temperature in an apartment'.

By the beginning of the twentieth century the use of cavity-wall construction in small houses was fairly common, but not yet normal. In 1905 rat-trap bond ('what is known in Surrey as garden wall bond') was recommended for economy, but the specification for a cottage costing £110 called for 'the brickwork of external walls to be 11-in hollow walls with galvanized iron ties at proper distances'.[9] Sometimes, as in plans for workers' cottages to be built at Penshurst, there were to be 'walls of double brick with air spaces between up to the first floor', with tiles hanging on 9-in brick above.[10] Generally the popularity of rendered walls at this time meant that the 9-in solid wall could remain in use with the added protection of the rendering, while presumably the low cost of coal meant that insulation was relatively unimportant. The cavity wall was still regarded as a cheap substitute rather than as a scientific design for economy.[11] In *Cassell's Building Construction*, published in weekly parts in 1905, Professor Adams was unenthusiastic about cavity-wall construction: 'cavity walls can hardly be said to be much used, when the number of buildings erected with solid walls is taken into account; but for detached country residences of two floors cavity walls are fairly frequent. It will be noted that the $4\frac{1}{2}$-in wall is in addition to the ordinary thickness; it would not answer to have two $4\frac{1}{2}$-in walls 2 in apart, connected by wall ties; these would certainly not be as strong as one 9-in wall.' *Rivington's Notes on Building Construction* was no more encouraging; the whole brickwork section in the 1915 edition had no illustration or description of cavity walling except a note that 'hollow walls of two $4\frac{1}{2}$ in thickness should be used only in single storey construction and with cement mortar'.[12] Even in the widely used Jaggard and Drury *Architectural Building Construction*, hollow walls were only mentioned in connection with damp-proofing stone walls in exposed situations.[13] Local by-laws must have remained unhelpful, for as late as 1923, in Edwin Gunn's *Little Things that Matter for those who build*, it was acknowledged that 'cavity wall construction' was being largely adopted in cheap building 'owing to the sanction of this form of construction by the latest model by-laws'.[14]

The great wave of small house building between the Wars, both for council tenants and for private clients, depended on cavity-wall construction. The technical section of the Tudor Walters Report, published in 1919 and forming the basis for the official housing manuals and much private housing policy, gave details of cavity-wall brickwork. The 1920 edition of *Mitchell's Building Construction* (Elementary) said that cavity walls 'are considerably and successfully used in many parts of England'.[15] By 1939 it was acknowledged, as in the article by L. H. Keay in Abercrombie's *Book of the Modern House*, that 'in general the $11\frac{1}{4}$-in brick cavity wall is the most satisfactory'.[16] The theoretical basis of cavity-wall construction was examined in the official *Principles of Modern Building* published in the previous year,[17] by which time the advantages were clearly understood and the precautions to be taken in design and construction using this technique were familiar to architect and builder alike. The cavity must be maintained; the base must be protected by a damp-proof course; the head must be open for ventilation but protected by the roof; where bridged by ties the cavity must be kept clear of mortar droppings; where interrupted by windows and doors the cavity must be protected by vertical and horizontal damp-proof courses and flashings; enough air bricks must be included to allow for evaporation of moisture but few enough to preserve the insulating properties of the air in the cavity.[18] Only the aesthetic problem remained insoluble; as the committee preparing the Post War Building Study No. 18, *The Architectural Use of Building Materials*, reported in 1946, 'Stretcher Bond is commonly used for the outer $4\frac{1}{2}$-in leaf of a cavity wall. It has a stupidly monotonous appearance and there must be many square miles of it all over the country.'[19] But their solution of using a bond of one snap header to three stretchers never found favour.

After 1945 cavity-wall construction once more became the basis of a housing drive, but by now both bricks and bricklayers were scarce, supplies undependable and skills expensive. Apart from the experiments in eliminating brick walls altogether, there were less well publicized but more significant experiments in using a cheaper, more quickly laid material for the inner leaf, where the bricklayer's skill was in any case less in evidence. Large 4-in thick blocks of coke-breeze and cement, made hollow to increase insulation and decrease weight, began to replace bricks in the inner leaf, and other comparable materials were also tried, so that by 1960 a cavity wall composed entirely of bricks was becoming unusual. Rising fuel costs and improving standards of comfort meant that the heat insulation properties of these blocks were at least as important as their quick and easy laying. Even this change was not sufficient and the cavity fill of foamed plastic or blown mineral wool became popular, gradually at first, and swiftly after the 1973 increase in oil prices.

By now the all-brick cavity wall has passed out of use. Only the outer leaf is of brick, the inner leaf is of insulating block and the cavity is often no longer a cavity but a third leaf of insulating material, a plastic fill between the permanent shuttering of the inner and outer leaves. There are doubts about this method of construction. Although theoretically unlikely it is in practice possible, in exposed situations and as a result of accidents or limitations of workmanship, for damp to penetrate along cracks in plastic-foam filling. The cavity may be restored as the barrier against dampness with reliance on the inner leaf for insulation and the outer leaf for stability and good appearance, or the inner leaf and the cavity may be replaced by some completely impervious insulating material. In either case the brick cavity wall as we have known it and as it was advocated for over a century before it came into general use will have gone for good.

NOTES

[1] William Atkinson, *Views of Picturesque Cottages with Plans*, London, 1805 (reprint Gregg Press, 1971), pp. 15–16. I am grateful to Grant Muter for the reference.

[2] Thomas Dearne, *Hints on an Improved Method of Building*, London, 1821.

[3] S. H. Brooks, *Designs for Cottage and Villa Architecture*, London, c. 1839, p. 59.

[4] H. Roberts, *The Dwellings of the Labouring Classes*, London, 1850, pp. 24–5.

[5] See T. Ritchie, 'Notes on the History of Hollow Masonry Walls', *Bulletin of the Association for Preservation Technology*, Vol. v, No. 4, 1973, pp. 40–9. The article is a most comprehensive review of cavity-wall construction in the United States and Canada.

[6] G. Vaux, *Villas and Cottages*, New York, 1867, pp. 76–7.

[7] J. J. Stevenson, *House Architecture* Vol. ii, London, 1880, pp. 172–4.

[8] J. Gwilt, *Encyclopaedia of Architecture* (Papworth edn), 1894, pp. 564–5 (paras 1902c and 2293a), and p. 1210.

[9] Home Counties, *How to Build or Buy a Country Cottage*, London, 1905, pp. 88–93 and p. 164.

[10] R. Williams and F. Knee, *The Labourer and his Cottage*, London, 1905, pp. 46–7 and p. 77.

[11] See H. B. Philpott, *Modern Cottages and Villas*, London, c. 1905, designs for small houses costing £150–£1,000, among others.

[12] W. N. Twelvetrees, *Rivington's Notes on Building Construction*, London, 1915, pp. 112 and 114.

[13] W. R. Jaggard and F. E. Drury, *Architectural Building Construction*, Vol. i, 1916, Vol. ii, 1923.

[14] Edwin Gunn, *Little Things that Matter for those who build*, London, 1923, p. 9.

[15] G. A. and A. M. Mitchell, *Building Construction and Drawing*, Vol. i, London, 1st edn 1911, p. 62.

[16] P. Abercrombie (ed.) *The Book of the Modern House*, London, 1939, p. 156.

[17] Department of Scientific and Industrial Research (Building Research Station), *Principles of Modern Building*, 1938.

[18] Although W. B. Mackay said of 'Cavity or Hollow Walls' that 'this type of construction is now very common and . . . is generally to be preferred to solid wall construction for many types of buildings, especially houses', he still felt it sufficiently advanced to be left to Volume II of his series *Building Construction* (London, 1944, pp. 40-4).

[19] *The Architectural Use of Building Materials*, Post War Building Study No. 18, by a Committee convened by the RIBA, London, 1946, p. 28.

Recording of Brickwork

Introduction

Full appreciation of our building heritage is bound to be helped by the understanding which comes from systematic observation. It is one of the delights of the study of brickwork that it can be done in any part of the town or countryside where bricks are to be found, that it can be done in odd moments as time and circumstances permit, and that it can be done quietly, unobtrusively, without impinging on the privacy of anyone, and with the minimum of equipment.

A procedure is recommended and a visual checklist provided whereby the characteristics of brickwork may be observed and recorded. The emphasis is on brickwork and not on the planning, construction, or architectural characteristics of a building. As brickwork may vary between front, side, and rear walls of a building, between a porch, bay or other ornamental feature and the rest of a building, and between the main walls and garden or boundary walls, one site may present many variations in the use of bricks but each part should be separately considered. The two pages of the visual checklist may be used simply as a pattern for observation or they may be used as the basis for a record form or pages in a record book.

Procedure

1. Identify the site – in the country by noting the name of the house, the parish and county; in the town by noting the street and number, the town and postal district or county.

2. Provide a grid reference which will locate the site even if it may not be precisely identified. In the country a reference of two letters and six figures will be enough; in the towns an eight-figure reference may be needed.

3. Give the site a serial number with an extra number for the part under consideration.

4. Identify the recorder and the date of record. A district may be covered by several people and interesting buildings are often altered and not infrequently demolished.

5. If a photograph is taken, then the spool and exposure number should be noted. One piece of brickwork can look very like another on a 35-mm negative.

6. Note the present use of the building and the original use if known.

7. Note the part being recorded: for example, the ornamental brick porch of an earlier house.

8. Note any dated feature: '1650 on chimney coping', '1715 on stone plaque built into brick wall', '1725 scored in a brick', etc.

9. Note the present state of the brickwork: for instance, is it substantially as original?

10. Note the surface condition of the brickwork: i.e. whether the bricks are exposed, whitewashed, rendered, etc.

11. Note the dimensions of the length, breadth, and thickness of a typical brick (several may have to be measured to ensure a representative example) and of the height of four bricks plus four joints. Dimensions should be in inches and millimetres.

12. Note the bond used or, in non-load-bearing panels, the brick pattern. Ignore the devices used by the bricklayer to meet the dimensions of the building; it is the bond which matters.

13. Note any pattern which shows on the building irrespective of the bonding: for example, the surface pattern of diaper work or the relief pattern of projecting headers.

14. Note the type of joint used, in the original jointing mortar or in any subsequent pointing.

15. Look at the architectural organization of the wall and note brickwork features of eaves, gable, string courses, etc.

16. Look at the openings – doorways, window apertures, etc. and note details at head, jamb and sill.

17. Quite often another building material is used with the brickwork, such as a stone lintel or sill to window openings, or a flint general walling material to which the brickwork gives decoration and reinforcement. These other materials should be noted against their positions of use.

18. Look at the chimney-stack and note the plan form – for instance, several square flues set diagonally – and the form of the cap; an example might be simple projecting brick courses. Ignore chimney-pots.

19. If the building is in fact of mathematical tiles and not of solid brickwork, then note the bond which is simulated and the wall and opening details.

20. Finally any other appropriate details should be noted and sketched.

The diagrams are intended to act as a visual checklist and a reminder of the meaning of the various terms used. The checklist is not comprehensive, for this would make it far too cumbersome; but it includes the features commonly found and provides for the uncommon features to be observed and recorded. On the facing page is a photograph of the building which was recorded on the checklist reproduced on pages 152 and 153.

1 Address of building			2 Grid reference	3 Serial
HESKETH ALMSHOUSES, HESLINGTON, YORKS, E.R			SE 663-495	10B

4 Surveyor RWB	5 Photo no.	6 Present use of building	7 Part recorded	8 Dated
Date SEPT 76	82/11	ALMSHOUSES	CENTREPIECE OF TERRACE	teature PLAQUE 1795
		Original use ALMS HOUSES		

9 Present state BUT REPAIRED
as original/~~altered~~/~~ruined~~/~~excavated~~/~~other~~

10 Surface condition
plain/~~glazed~~/~~painted~~/~~washed~~/~~rendered~~/~~other~~

11 Dimensions
8¾/220   4⅜/110   2⅜/60   10¼"/260mm

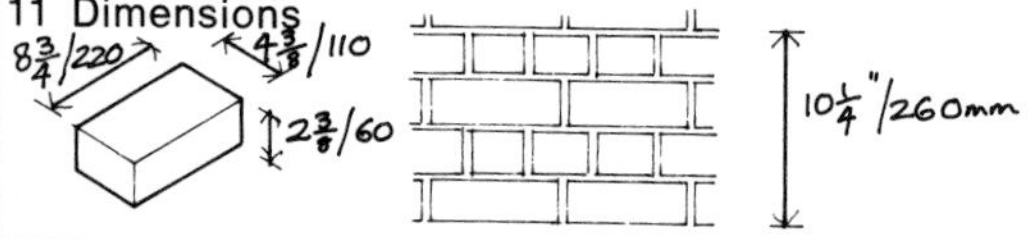

12 Bond

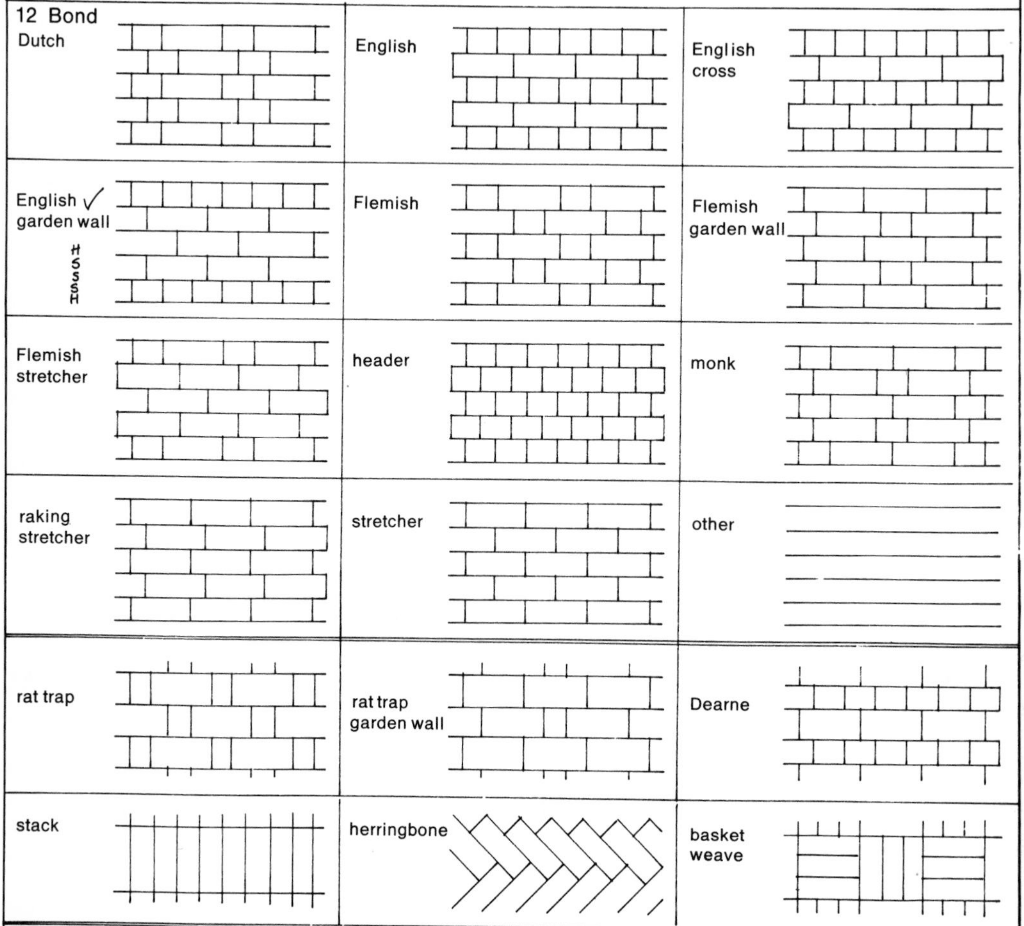

Dutch

English

English cross

English garden wall ✓
H
S
S
H

Flemish

Flemish garden wall

Flemish stretcher

header

monk

raking stretcher

stretcher

other

rat trap

rat trap garden wall

Dearne

stack

herringbone

basket weave

13 Pattern NONE

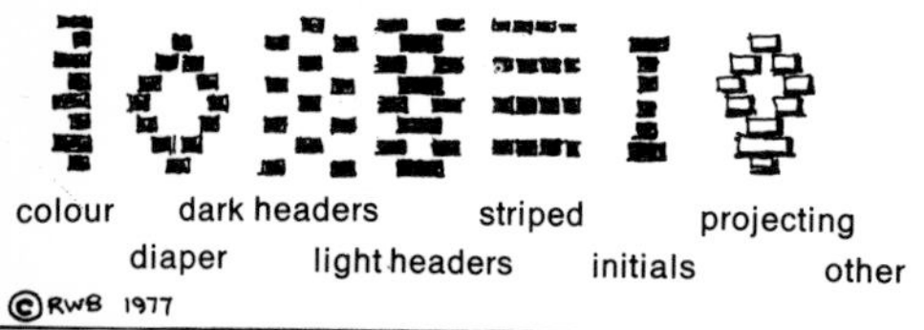

colour   dark headers   striped   projecting
diaper   light headers   initials   other

© RWB 1977

14 Jointing

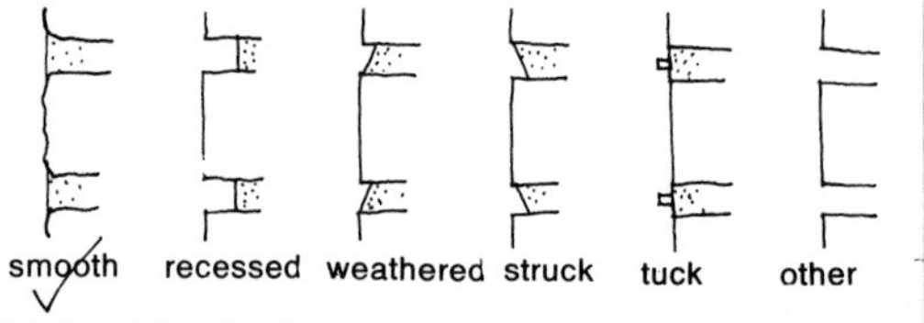

smooth ✓   recessed   weathered   struck   tuck   other

15 Walling

PEDIMENT, DENTILS AT BASE OF GABLE OVERSAILING COURSE AT VERGE

	1	2	3	4	5	other
a eaves	plain	oversail	dentil ✓	dog-tooth	moulded	other
b gable	plain	Dutch	corbie-step	tumbling	b. on edge	other ✓
c coping	b. on edge	terracotta	moulded	rubbed		✓ STONE other
d string	project	dentil	dog-tooth	inset	moulded	— other
e plinth	plain	splayed	moulded	terracotta		— other
f quoins	plain	coloured	projecting			— other

16 Openings

ROUGH RING AROUND CARTOUCHE IN PEDIMENT

	1	2	3	4	5	other
a head	flat ✓	soldier	b. on edge	on frame	cambered	other
b arch	semicircular	elliptical	segmental	moulded	pointed	— other
c voussoirs	uncut	cut ✓	gauged	moulded	terracotta	other
d jamb	plain ✓	rubbed	moulded			other
e sill	plain	b. on edge	gauged	moulded	terracotta	✓ STONE other
f apron	plain	shaped				— other

17 Other materials

	stone	flint	cobble	clay	other
a walling					
b plinth					
c quoins					
d head					
e arch					
f jamb					
g other SILLS	✓				

18 Chimney-stack

plan

PLAIN RECTANGULAR

capping

DOUBLE COURSE OVERSAILING

19 Mathematical tiles

		corner detail
header		
stretcher		
Flemish		head detail
English		
other		

20 Other details

BLIND WINDOW OVER DOOR, CONTAINS PLAQUE

© RWB 1977

Bibliography

Apart from textbooks of building construction very few books have been written about brickwork in England nor have many articles been written on the subject. The following list of a dozen or so items includes some of the works which have proved useful in the preparation of this book. For further references to specific items the reader is directed to the bibliography which is to be published by the British Brick Society and for further examples of the use of brickwork in buildings the volumes of the *Buildings of England* series by Sir Nikolaus Pevsner and others are invaluable.

N. Davey, *A History of Building Materials*, 1961

N. Lloyd, *A History of English Brickwork*, 1925

C. C. Handisyde and B. A. Haseltine, *Bricks and Brickwork*, 1975

W. B. McKay, *Building Construction*, Vol. I 2nd edn 1943, Vol. II 1944, *Brickwork*, 2nd edn 1968

G. and A. Mitchell, *Building Construction*, Part I, 18th edn 1946

John Prizeman, *Your House : The Outside View*, 1975

L. F. Salzman, *Building in England down to 1540*, 1952

Jane Wight, *Brick Building in England from the Middle Ages to 1550*, 1972

John Woodforde, *Bricks to Build a House*, 1976

Anthea Brian, 'A regional survey of brick bonding in England and Wales', *Vernacular Architecture* (Journal of the Vernacular Architecture Group), Vol. III, 1972, pp. 11–15

E. Dobson, 'A Rudimentary Treatise on the Manufacture of Bricks and Tiles', published 1850 and reprinted with an introduction by F. Celoria in *Journal of Ceramic History*, No. 5, 1971

L. S. Harley, 'A typology of brick: with numerical coding of brick characteristics', *Journal of the British Archaeological Association*, 3rd Series, Vol. XXXVIII, 1974

D. L. Roberts, 'Recording Vernacular Architecture in a wide field', *East Midlands Regional Bulletin of Local History*, 8, 1973

T. P. Smith, 'Rye House, Hertfordshire, and Aspects of Early Brickwork in England', *The Archaeological Journal*, Vol. 132, 1976

Index